THE
ROMANS

John Manley

ALL THAT
MATTERS

Contents

Introduction

In 2012 an unusual planning application was received by the Forest of Dean District Council in the west of England. It was submitted by a hedge fund manager who had made a fortune by betting on the outcomes of various financial investments. He wanted to spend his nest egg on building a chicken coop in his garden, but not just any old coop: this was to be a 72 m^2 edifice constructed mostly from local stone. Plans and elevations submitted show that the coop drew its inspiration from the classical world. It would resemble a temple: steps up to a stone podium, fluted columns, Ionic capitals and a triangular pedimented roof, complete with antefixes, carved ornaments terminating in lines of tiles on the roof edge. One or two chickens were shown at the foot of the columns on the elevation drawings, apparently quite at home.

There are two things that are interesting about this story. One is rather obvious and relates to the construction itself. Leaving aside the question as to whether this is a sensible use of money, the classical styling of the building clearly demonstrates the powerful magnetism of Graeco-Roman civilisation for some Western Europeans. Clearly this hedge fund manager wanted to make a statement to his neighbours, or to his family, or to his chickens – or perhaps to all three. But there is a more subtle point: maybe the manager was fulfilling a vow. Chickens were raised by priests in ancient Rome to foretell the future, and no significant military action was undertaken without consulting the sacred chickens for favourable omens. They were fed grain: if they ate it vigorously the signs were good, but if they refused to eat and drink then the auguries were bad and any decisions or military actions were postponed. Roman naval commander Claudius Pulcher famously lost a battle in the first Punic war by ignoring the fact that the chickens had refused to eat, furiously throwing them into the sea so that they could at least drink. Modern international finance is equally frustrating to many of us. So how had this fund manager been so successful? Had he been more interested in whether his chickens fed than in consuming their eggs? Was this the secret underlying the success of his financial wheeling and dealing? Was the temple-coop the chickens' pay-off – a sort of 'thanks for the tip'?

There is no doubt that the Romans have an appeal, a hold even, on some of us. The number of books, novels, TV series, museum exhibitions and websites is evidence of the re-interpretation and re-working of Roman history and archaeology by successive generations, and each has its own opinions on the importance of the Romans. There is perhaps no other ancient people that exerts such an influence on us. A qualification is required here on the 'us' in the last few sentences. It is quite easy to equate unconsciously the easy use of 'us' with inhabitants of the Western world, but in the ancient world there was a schism between a Latin West and a Greek East, not least because a new Rome, Constantinople, eventually usurped its Italian predecessor. Readers will be aware that multiple and sometimes contentious differences still exist between East and West, most obviously demonstrated by the differing beliefs and practices of the Islamic and Christian religions. In present day Islamic countries in North Africa and the Middle East, those whose territories were once incorporated within the Roman empire, that fascination with all things Roman is more muted. We will return to this point later, but for the time being let us focus on what exactly it is about the Romans that has produced this enduring fascination, this curiosity that is more prevalent in the West.

At the height of its supremacy, around 130 CE under Emperor Hadrian, the Roman empire consisted of some five to six million km², inhabited by approximately 60 to 70 million people who comprised between a quarter and a sixth of the world's population.

Then the Empire stretched from Hadrian's Wall in drizzle-soaked northern England to the sun-baked banks of the Euphrates in Syria; from the great Rhine-Danube river system, which snaked across the fertile, flat lands of Europe from the Low Countries to the Black Sea, to the rich plains of the North African coast and the luxuriant gash of the Nile Valley in Egypt. The Empire completely circled the Mediterranean ... referred to by its conquerors as mare nostrum – 'our sea'

(Kelly, C, 2006., The Roman Empire, p. 1).

That sweeping description is impressive enough, especially if you remember that the origins of Rome at the beginning of the last millennium BCE lay in some villages of timber, daub and thatch scattered across a few hills of tufa on the left bank of the Tiber in central Italy. But when you recall that Rome's expansion and ascendancy lasted over 1,000 years the phenomenon of the Romans becomes scarcely believable.

The brevity of this particular book concentrates the attention on the things that really matter about the Romans without obscuring the significant themes with too much historical detail. It aims to be a springboard from which the reader can delve deeper into any particular aspect. First we will explore the legacy of the Romans: the various aspects of Roman culture and society that have become important to the modern world. The second crucial question concerns the causes of Roman expansion. What drove their seemingly incessant need to make war and make other peoples subservient? The third issue examines the rulers themselves. Who made up the minority ruling classes? Who brought stability and kept order in the far-flung provinces? Our fourth point for discussion is the masses, the dominated, the poor. What did they think about being imperial subjects? Indeed, did all of them realize that they were? Penultimately we will look at 'material culture', by which I mean the obvious tangible things from architecture and artworks to everyday pots and pans. The Romans were probably the first mass producers and exporters of tableware for the home. What effect did the rise of consumerism have on one quarter of the ancient world? Finally, there is the fall. What combination of factors led to the decline and ultimate extinction of perhaps the greatest ancient empire the world has ever known?

Before we start it is important to recognize the potential bias in our sources and in ourselves. To begin with the sources, most of what we know, or think we know, about the Romans stems from two sorts of evidence: the classical texts that have survived, and archaeological discoveries. Neither is objective. Classical authors by and large wrote for the elite of Roman society and were likely to comment on aspects of government, society or warfare that a privileged and educated audience would find interesting. Nor were classical historians necessarily interested in portraying an unvarnished account of things that had happened.

Archaeologists have been no less partisan. Partly this is a product of the differential survival of archaeological evidence: solid, large things such as stone columns from a rich villa survive best, while organic, smaller things such as clothing are preserved less well. Partisanship may also be due to the tendency of archaeologists to concentrate on spectacular Roman remains – the ruins of Pompeii, Jerash in Jordan, large military forts, impressive villas – sometimes at the cost of less appealing sites such as the small homes of tenant farmers on some unproductive lands on the outskirts of Empire. This present book is based upon the research of countless modern scholars of the Roman world; it would have been impossible without their efforts. But they all probably have their biases, small or great, things they are fundamentally drawn to, things that they consider significant. I know I have.

The Roman legacy

That the Romans left a legacy has entered popular consciousness. In fact, 'What did the Romans ever do for us?' has even become a bit of a cliché, no doubt helped to such lofty cultural status by the famous line in Monty Python's *Life of Brian*, which points out in reply to this very question that they brought sanitation, medicine, education, viniculture, public order, irrigation, roads, the fresh-water system and public health!

An impressive list, and the Romans did indeed bring all of these things, and more, to many regions around the Mediterranean. If we are to examine the Roman legacy then we need to identify those key features, some of them material, some abstract concepts, that inform contemporary society. We also need to understand how those things and concepts were transmitted from the ancient world to the twenty-first century.

▶ Beware of Greeks bearing gifts...

First, however, it is important to remember that the Romans were in receipt of a legacy themselves: that of the Greeks. Opinions differ on how much of the cultural output of Rome was developed under the shadow of Greece. The Roman poet Horace famously wrote that Greece had made a captive of her conqueror, bringing the arts to the hillbillies of Latium (Horace, *Epistles*, 2.1. 156). Virgil opined that the Greeks achieved higher mastery in arts and sciences, while the Romans excelled in the more practical skills of conquest and good government (Virgil, *Aeneid*, 6. 847-53). The Romans themselves, therefore, had some ideas about what the Romans, as opposed to others, were good at; indeed rather better at. Strabo, himself a Greek, wrote:

> The Greeks are famous for their cities and in this they aimed at beauty. The Romans excelled in those things which the Greeks took little interest in such as the building of roads, aqueducts and sewers

(*Strabo*, Geography, *Book V, Chapter 3*).

Overt anti-Greek sentiments also feature in the work of water commissioner Frontinus, perhaps the typical view of an engineer:

> Compare such important engineering works carrying so much water with the idle pyramids and the useless though famous buildings of the Greeks ... Water is brought into the city through aqueducts in such quantities that it is like a river flowing through the city

(*Frontinus*, De aquae urbis Romae, *16*).

In some measure these writers were correct. The Romans have been viewed as both an imitative and a technically very practical people.

▶ The political legacy

One of the most enduring legacies of the Romans was in the field of politics. Two political models derive from Rome itself: the 'mixed constitution' of the middle and late republic, and the more autocratic rule sometimes described as 'Caesarism'. Until the fall of the republic in the first century BCE, Rome was governed by a large group of aristocrats, which periodically consented to recruit new members into its midst, and which met as the senate. Public offices were held for one year at a time, and election was by a complicated system that allowed the whole citizen body to take part, although the outcomes were usually weighted in favour of the wealthier classes. Greek observers such as the historian Polybius described this as a 'mixed constitution', while Cicero was self-congratulatory, arguing that the Roman system avoided the extremes of democracy and oligarchy that had weakened Greece. Cicero's concept of natural law, determined by nature and thus universal, obliged his fellow citizens to contribute to the general good of the society, governed by an elite on their behalf. This concept had a profound effect on the development of political thought in the Western world. It was constantly quoted in the Middle Ages and taken up by liberal thinkers such as John Locke, who subsequently significantly influenced Thomas Jefferson. A classical ancestry thus underlies some of the principles of the United States Declaration of Independence as well as its constitution. It also underlies most Western-style democracies, whether practised at national, regional or local level.

The other political model bequeathed by Rome is named after Julius Caesar, who was proclaimed Dictator for ten years in 46 BCE. His elevation came at a time of Republican crisis. Government had become dysfunctional in the first century BCE, in part because Rome's campaigning generals had amassed huge financial fortunes and were backed by armies more loyal to them than to the senate, and in part because the senate became dominated by a much narrower political elite. Caesar's dictatorship was anathema to Republican diehards, however, and Caesar was assassinated in 44 BCE. Republican government was never restored and after a lengthy and brutal period of civil war monarchical government eventually emerged under Augustus. The legacy of Caesarism has been a durable one. At the start of the sixteenth century Pope Julius II, 'the warrior Pope', named himself after Julius Caesar. At the beginning of the twentieth century there were still three rulers who bore the name Caesar: the German and Austrian Kaisers and the Russian Czar. But the Roman legacy was not the creation of monarchy – for there had been many monarchs before Rome, especially in ancient kingdoms of the Middle East – but the combination of absolutism regulated by a highly developed system of law.

Another crucially important political aspect of the legacy was the institution of Roman citizenship. 'Roman' was a legal term and anyone, of any race, could become a Roman citizen. This was a remarkably liberal arrangement and it struck the Greeks themselves as such as early as the third century BCE. King Philip V of Macedon noted that the Romans were so free with the gift of citizenship that they sometimes granted it even to former slaves. Citizenship brought many rights and privileges, including immunity from some taxes and the right to have a trial under Roman law. A Roman citizen could not be tortured or whipped, nor could he receive the death penalty, unless he was found guilty of treason. An edict of Emperor Caracalla in 212 CE massively extended citizenship to all free men in the empire, and all free women were to enjoy the same rights as Roman women. Citizenship was therefore liberally utilized by Roman emperors to bring a sense of belonging and cohesion to the empire, although in the century after Caracalla's initiative a new legal distinction emerged between the *humiliores* (lower classes) and the *honestiores* (upper classes). The idea of an empire-wide citizenship had a significant and lasting effect on Western Europe long after the demise of the Romans. It enhanced a feeling of a shared cultural unity which underlay the later creation of Charlemagne's Christian empire in 800 CE and the Holy Roman Empire from 962 CE onwards. This unity did not survive in the Middle East, nor in North Africa where the Arab conquests of the seventh and eighth centuries CE created a different cohesion based on faith and language.

▶ The architectural legacy

More tangible aspects of the Roman legacy lie in buildings. The achievements of ancient Rome in planning, building and decoration underlie many of the principal developments of Western architecture. With a moment's reflection most of us can remember some modern edifice whose columns and capitals recall the temples of ancient Rome. There is an important qualification, however: whereas most of our neo-classical buildings exhibit the simplicity of stone in all its natural colours, those of the ancient world were often partially or completely painted in what we would consider garish polychrome. Tastes, as well as times, change. The Roman architect, engineer and scholar Vitruvius wrote an architectural treatise in the first century BCE; the only one to survive in its entirety from antiquity. For Vitruvius the city was the natural focus of an ordered and civilized life, and the *forum* the prime locus for public and commercial activities.

Basilicas should be constructed on a site adjoining the forum and in the warmest possible quarter, so that in winter businessmen may gather in them without being troubled by the weather

(*Vitruvius*, De Architectura, *Book V, I, 2).*

The legalization of Christianity by Emperor Constantine in 313 CE created the opportunity for the construction of countless churches. Constantine chose the basilica form as his model for early churches; traditional temples had too many pagan connotations and offered no place for a congregation. The basilica was adopted by Charlemagne for a throne-hall, and was revived in the Romanesque architecture of the eleventh and twelfth centuries and in Renaissance Florence, in such churches as San Lorenzo (1421) and Santo Spirito (1436). The form continued in secular use, for instance in the York Assembly Rooms of 1730, a theatrical interior of Corinthian columns and bays which hosted dances and other entertainments for the city's elite; it also tends to be reflected to this day in many Roman Catholic churches erected in Britain since the mid-nineteenth century.

The monumental baths of Rome, such as those of Caracalla and Diocletian, provided the inspiration for a number of influential architects, including Andreas Palladio in the sixteenth century. They studied the planning of bath buildings – a complex arrangement of domed rooms, halls, apses and courtyards – and applied the lessons learnt to their own designs. Use of these architectural principles produced some of the finest neo-classical buildings in modern times, such as St George's Hall in Liverpool which opened for public use in 1854. Surrounded by impressive files of columns, it was a truly multi-purpose building from the start: people could be tried for murder, listen to a concert or attend a ball, all under one roof. The highly unusual plan of St George's drew inspiration from the *frigidarium*, *tepidarium* and

▲ Old Pennsylvania Station, New York; a recreation of the Baths of Caracalla in Rome.

caldarium of the Baths of Caracalla. But the greatest ever tribute to those baths was undoubtedly the old Pennsylvania Station, New York City. A vaulted waiting room was modelled on the Caracallan *tepidarium*, but with dimensions increased by 20 per cent. Its steel frame was clad externally in Roman travertine, quarried near Tivoli. The adjacent concourse was an even more daring adaptation of the thermal theme: three high vaults, protruding from the main mass of the structures, were constructed of steel and glass. Penn Station really was ancient Rome come to Manhattan. Not surprisingly, its demolition in 1963 caused an international storm:

Until the first blow fell, no one was convinced that Penn Station really would be demolished, or that New York would permit this monumental act of vandalism against one of the largest and finest landmarks of its age of Roman elegance

(New York Times, October 30th, 1963).

The triumphal arch is another leitmotif of the Roman legacy. Originally temporary structures erected by magistrates on festive occasions to celebrate the victories of military heroes, by the end of the first century BCE they had become monumental and richly carved gateways of stone. Triumphal arches were a most easily recognized symbol of Roman power and order. The most visited in Rome are those of Emperors Titus and Septimius Severus, at either end of the forum, and that of Constantine, next to the Colosseum. Not surprisingly, given the imperial associations of the triumphal arch, this form of monument was commissioned by some of Europe's rulers both to proclaim and legitimize their power. The Arc du Carrousel on the site of the former Tuileries Palace in Paris was erected between 1806 and 1808; it commemorated military victories of Napoleon, including his entrance into Munich and Vienna. The arch was based on that of Septimius Severus. Another famous example can be seen in London's Marble Arch. Built of white Cararra marble, it was originally designed as a ceremonial gateway to Buckingham Palace, and was intended to carry sculpted reliefs depicting British victories during the Napoleonic Wars; it was based on the Arch of Constantine.

The Pantheon in Rome, a temple to all the gods, was rebuilt by Emperor Hadrian in 126 CE. A centrally planned building, it combined a huge circular domed room with an *oculus*, or eye-to-the-sky, and was fronted by three rows of granite columns with Corinthian capitals. As one of the most complete survivals from antiquity the building has been immensely influential and its essential components of portico and dome have appeared in a number of universities, city halls, public libraries as well as country houses such as the Villa Rotunda, just outside Vicenza. In the USA Thomas Jefferson drew on the familiar religious monuments of ancient Rome to legitimize the new American Republic. The early imperial Roman temple at Nîmes, now known as the Maison Carrée, was in 1775 the model for his new State Capitol at Richmond, Virginia. The library dominating his university in the same state at Charlottesville was one of the most reverberant of echoes of the Pantheon. Appropriately, the Jefferson Memorial in Washington, built 1939 to 1943, evokes the Pantheon in its design. Never completed was Hitler's and Albert Speer's idea of a huge domed building for his *Volkshalle* (People's Hall) based on the Pantheon which the former had visited in 1938. A record survives of the lasting impression it made on him:

From the time I experienced this building – no description, picture or photograph did it justice – I became interested in its history [...] For a short while I stood in this space (the rotunda) – what majesty! I gazed at the large open oculus and saw the universe and sensed what had given this space the name Pantheon – God and the world are one

(See http://en.wikipedia.org/wiki/Volkshalle#
Hitler_and_Hadrian.27s_Pantheon).

Roman domestic architecture too has left its legacy. Inevitably the excavations at Pompeii and Herculaneum, from the mid-eighteenth century, have provided a rich corpus of houses, while the sprawling arrangements of the ruins of Hadrian's villa at Tivoli – disparate buildings linked by canals, pools, colonnades and fountains and embellished with open-air sculpture – have continually fascinated architects. In the nineteenth century Napoleon III commissioned a Pompeian house for his Parisian residence at 18, Avenue de Montaigne, though sadly this is no longer in existence. An ambitious recreation of an antique villa constructed originally in the 1970s is the J. Paul Getty Museum at the Getty Villa, Malibu in California, based on the Villa of the Papyri at Herculaneum. One of its highlights is the outer peristyle, complete with *piscina*, gardens and outdoor sculpture.

▶ Latin and law

We have looked at two main components – one ideological, one material – of the Roman legacy, and noted how they have influenced modern Western thought and practice. However, the legacy of Rome was, and is, much more multi-faceted. Latin was central to the development of Romance languages, including French, Italian, Spanish, Portuguese and Romanian. There is a shared stock of lexical and grammatical items in these that is virtually entirely of Latin origin. Even in a non-Romance language as English, it has been estimated that over a quarter of its vocabulary ultimately derives from Latin. The Latin alphabet has become one of the most widely accepted all over the world and the Romans encouraged literacy in Latin among the elite, particularly in the Western provinces. Recognizable lines of Virgil's *Aeneid* have been found across the Empire as graffiti, testament to widespread if basic literacy. The Latin works of most classical authors, which had survived the collapse of Rome through safekeeping in ecclesiastical libraries, were transcribed during the Carolingian empire of Charlemagne.

In the Eastern provinces Greek remained the language of culture for educated Romans. Greek works of other scholars in the empire, such as those of Galen of Pergamon (in modern-day Turkey), a prominent Roman of Greek ethnicity, physician, surgeon and philosopher of the second century CE, survived partly because of Islamic interest. They were first translated into Arabic, and from the eleventh century onwards from Arabic back into Latin in the West.

Roman law, codified by the Eastern emperor Justinian in the sixth century CE, formed the basis of many European legal systems until the early 1800s. It also formed the foundation for legal systems in the Americas, Australia, New Zealand and post-1945 Japan. Although no longer practised, its provisions are still indispensible for understanding civil law today. Roman law may have lacked notions similar to modern-day human rights, but it did consist of an impressive framework for regulating family, property and people's dealings with one another. How Justinian's Digest, the most important part of his codification, survived is still a mystery. It was extant in a sixth-century manuscript which reappeared in Pisa in the 1070s CE. In 1406 the Florentines carried it off as war booty and it has remained in their city until the present day.

▶ The idea of empire

One of the most significant legacies was the way in which the multiple stories of the Roman empire, and the idea of imperialism itself, were adopted and manipulated by the emerging nations of Western Europe. It was a case of the classical past serving the needs of the early modern present. Communities in the Italian peninsula drew upon the Roman imperial past as a golden age of prosperity from the Middle Ages onward. In the Italy of the 1700s, when the peninsula was a mosaic of small independent states or city states, ancient Rome was extolled not as a power that repressed autonomy, but as an overarching authority that allowed a federation of autonomous communities to thrive. However, in the nineteenth century when Italy was unified the Romans were recast as lauded unifiers. Before WWII fascism used Roman symbols to draw a congruence between the armies of Rome and those of Mussolini. Italian colonial projects proclaimed a direct link with a presumed ancient heritage. Italian stamps in Libya bore the motto 'we are back'.

Political involvement of Spain in Italy from the fifteenth century onwards assisted the import of Roman ideology. The Catholic monarchs thought of themselves as inheritors of the Roman empire, claiming a direct ancestry, through the Visigothic kings, to the emperors. Trajan, after all, was Iberian in origin, albeit probably from an immigrant Italian family. Charles III authorized investigative works on the Vesuvian cities, many books on Roman architecture were printed in Spain, and Seville was proclaimed the 'New Rome'.

The peoples whom the Romans conquered, known from classical authors, provided a contrasting native or indigenous identity to the conquerors. Gauls, Batavians, Britons, Germans and Dacians were all stereotyped as significant ethnic groups by writers such as Tacitus and Cassius Dio. These rebellious ancient 'others' were occasionally repackaged to help define and unite the citizens of individual nations in Western Europe. Growing nationalistic aspirations among the Germans in the nineteenth century found encouragement in the exploits of Arminius (a.k.a. 'Hermann the German'), leader of the Cherusci, in the Teutoberg Forest. Three Roman legions had been annihilated in 9 CE and Rome's adventures east of the Rhine suffered with them. Arminius/Hermann became a national hero, despite the question mark over his German credentials, as he was certainly a Roman citizen. The Hermann euphoria resulted in the development of many Hermann societies which raised money for a classical sculpture of their hero. After 1871 France became the enemy. Hermann now stood alongside Kaiser Wilhelm as a liberator from the Gallic oppressors.

In France, Hermann's opponent in the emerging nations stakes was Vercingetorix, a prominent tribal leader who fought Julius Caesar. He soon established an alliance with other tribes and took control of their combined armies, leading them in Gaul's most significant revolt against Roman power. However, Vercingetorix surrendered to Caesar after being defeated at the Battle of Alesia in 52 BCE. He was then imprisoned for five years, until in 46 BCE he was paraded through Rome as part of Caesar's triumph before being executed.

Post-revolutionary France latched onto Vercingetorix as the perfect vehicle to promote emerging Gallic nationalism. It has to be said the Hermann versus Vercingetorix match-up was a godsend to political ideologists either side of the Rhine. However, the waters were a little muddied by the intellectual leanings of Napoleon III. Both he and his uncle, Napoleon (I) Bonaparte, were admirers of Caesar and wrote commentaries on his Gallic Wars as a way of bolstering French imperial inclinations. Napoleon III turned his attention to excavations at Alesia, concentrating on Caesar's siege-works and completely ignoring the hillfort that the siege works surrounded where Vercingetorix and his Gaulish defenders made their last stand. An unavoidable dilemma ensued. Napoleon wished to erect a commemorative statue at the site – but to which hero? Heart ruled over head and a statue of Vercingetorix was duly unveiled. The inscription at its base read:

United Gaul, in a single nation, fired by a single spirit, can defy the world. Napoleon III, Emperor of the French, in memory of Vercingetorix.

The message was clear. A resurrected Vercingetorix would lead an imperial France forward. His cultural legacy included the cartoon characters Asterix and Obelix, wily Gauls forever getting one over the dim-witted Romans.

For Britain the imperialism of Rome was reworked through the British Empire, particularly in the period between 1880 and 1930. A well-defined image of Roman Britain developed in the later nineteenth century as a historical parallel for British India. Under this guise the ancient Britons or 'Celts' played the part of the Indian population, while the Roman officers were the British commanding classes in the subcontinent. Both Roman and British officials shared a mission to 'civilize' the indigenous. But just as in France two competing but still coexistent ideologies emerged, one foregrounding the Romans as imperial torchbearers, the other flagging up native resistance to them. In the early twentieth century various writers provided dramatic renditions of the revolt of Boudica, leader of the Iceni (a tribe that once occupied part of eastern England), against the Romans. This strand of national resistance was memorialized in the statue of a defiant Boudica in a chariot on the Embankment beside Westminster Bridge in London.

▶ The legacy in East and West

The Roman legacy seems more fundamental to Western Europe than to the Middle East or North Africa and there are reasons for that, briefly noted here. Some of these reasons have their roots in the classical period. While the Romans could perceive themselves as superior to the 'barbarians' of the West, that was not so easy in the East, where educated Romans were in thrall to the sophistication of Greek culture, and to the long histories and great cities of kingdoms around the eastern end of the Mediterranean. The early conquests of Islam in the seventh and eighth centuries CE in the East and North Africa, the confrontation of religions effected through the crusades, the eventual fall of Constantinople in 1453 and the different linguistic inheritances meant that the two halves of the former Roman Empire developed in dramatically different ways in the early modern period, as indeed they had since the late fifth century.

While the emerging nations of the West could harness and manipulate their classical heritage to positive effect, Arab nationalism stressed the potential unity of the Arab world, united by Islam and the Arabic language, rejecting Western practices seen as unnatural and corrupt. In North Africa the great ruins of cities left by the Romans were seen as too closely associated with the Western imperial powers of France and Italy, both of which colonized regions of the North African littoral. Classical ruins could thus be easily viewed as unwelcome reminders of a more recent, un-free past. Modern tourism, supported by Islamic governments, has mainly targeted Western holidaymakers, quite successfully. Inevitably the insensitive activities of some Western tourists visiting ancient sites can upset local communities; yet another reason for local Islamic communities to consider heritage tourism a mixed blessing. The overall picture is not a monochrome one, however. Outside the site museum at Lepcis Magna, a Roman city in Libya, a defiant statue of Emperor Septimius Severus, born in Lepcis, proclaims that he is an African Emperor of Rome, a clear sign of an official attempt to claim ownership of the country's pre-Islamic, Roman legacy.

Syrian attitudes in particular are influenced hugely by awareness of their own Roman legacy. Philip the Arab, a third-century emperor born east of the Sea of Galilee, appears on their banknotes, while they view the 'Roman' remains of Palmyra – perhaps rightly – in terms of something almost solely Syrian. In Turkey, very different from the Arab world, a huge amount of money has been spent on preserving and interpreting classical ruins. It also advertises its Graeco-Roman legacy by naming a national beer after Ephesus.

▶ And finally...

Regrettably we must pass over additional Roman influences, which have been beneficial to most of the creative arts, especially sculpture, drama and poetry. But let us pause to consider Shakespeare studying Latin grammar as a youngster in Stratford-upon-Avon. In some of his plays the present was read through the lens of the classical past, even if they were sometimes confused. Thus there is a reference to un-Roman 'chimney pots' in *Julius Caesar*, the eponymous hero also held erroneously responsible for the building of the Tower of London (*Richard II*, 5.1.2). Christianity was also a significant part of the Roman legacy, although it is easy to forget that it began as an Eastern cult subsequently infiltrating a polytheistic universe. And a whole series of Roman inventions have come down to us, comprising, *inter alia*, military formations and armour, medical instruments, a shared coinage (akin to the euro), the first widespread use of glass and all those aqueducts, roads and sewers. Last but not least, there is a humble product abundant today, and one which typifies the Roman strength of character: concrete. We do not have to consult chickens to guess that there is probably some near to every reader.

If the Roman legacy has been so far-reaching, accepted by some and shunned by others, we need to retrace our footsteps back to where it all began and ask the very simple question – just how did Rome come to control a quarter of the known world?

2

Romans as conquerors

The Romans excelled at numerous things, but if there is one paperback image that is often called to mind when thinking about them it is the hard-bitten legionary soldier, all muscle, stubble and unsheathed sword, who symbolizes the all-conquering might of Rome. But where did that fighting spirit come from? What drove Rome to conquer, and then conquer again? What was special about the Romans?

▶ Romulus and Remus

The story of Rome's foundation is mythical and unverifiable, only written down by classical historians at a much later date. Twins Romulus (after whom Rome was named) and Remus are central to our story. Both were supposedly descended from Aeneas, fugitive from

▲ The myth of Rome's foundation: a she-wolf suckling Romulus and Remus.

Troy (in western Anatolia) after its destruction by the Greeks, according to the version given by Plutarch. As babies the twins were perceived as a threat to the king of Alba Longa, an ancient town south-east of Rome, and thus condemned to death. Pitied by a servant, they were placed in a basket and left to float down the Tiber, where, near the Palatine Hill, they were rescued from a swamp (having been fortunately fed by a she-wolf and a woodpecker) and then raised by a local family of shepherds.

However, the twins, prone to sibling rivalry, were born to lead men not sheep. As adults Romulus wanted to found a city on the Palatine, Remus one on the Aventine. They resolved to consult the auguries, quarrelled over their interpretation, and Romulus killed his twin brother. The new city, traditionally founded in 753 BCE, grew rapidly; it filled with listless, landless, mostly male immigrants, so Romulus launched an attack on the Sabines, a people in the central Apennines, abducting many of their women to provide wives for his followers. Eventually Sabines and Romans were joined as one people: the Romans.

Origin myth though this may be, there are themes in it that recur in later Roman history. One is the singular importance of families, and how their organization and development, and the feuds and alliances both in and between them, dominated the politics of the capital. The second is ruthlessness and violence. The third concerns the significance of spoils of war, in this case women. The fourth highlights the ability of Rome to incorporate a defeated opponent, to make them Romans too, through a variety of different types of political affiliation.

▶ From kings to senators

For the first couple of centuries of its existence Rome was ruled by kings. One of them, Servius Tullius, re-organized the army and was the first to provide the city with a defensive wall, sometime in the middle of the sixth century BCE. His successor, Lucius Tarquinius Superbus, the latter word meaning 'arrogant or lofty', was proud but not so popular. Originally of Etruscan origin, he ruled in an autocratic and tyrannical manner; he and his family were exiled from Rome after a popular uprising. Out of this revolution the Roman republic was born, traditionally in 509 BCE. Rome was to be governed no more by kings, but by elected magistrates and the senate.

The republicans soon had heroes to inspire the new political arrangements. When the Etruscan kings were trying to re-establish their ascendancy in Rome, Horatius virtually single-handedly kept the invaders at bay on a bridge over the Tiber, as the bridge was dismantled behind him. Thomas Macaulay's 1842 poem *Horatius* paints a dramatic picture:

Oh Tiber, father Tiber, to whom the Romans pray,

A Roman's life, a Roman's arms, take thou in charge this day!

So he spake and, speaking, sheathed the good sword by his side,

He swam back safely, naturally enough, and was granted land near the city and a statue in his honour.

Some cognizance of the city of Rome's wider place in the Italian and Mediterranean world must have developed fairly quickly in the republic since there is an early tradition of the city's alliance with Carthage, on the North African coast. In 496 BCE Rome is also supposed to have defeated an alliance of local tribes led by the exiled King Tarquinius, some 20 km east of the city. But two pivotal events of the early fourth century BCE – a victory and a near-catastrophe – helped steer the collective Roman psyche towards what could loosely be described as a mentality of aggressive expansionism.

The enmity between the Etruscans and the Romans simmered from the time of the kings onwards. For over a century Rome and its nearest Etruscan neighbour, the city of Veii, had traded insults across the Tiber – at least three wars and two truces were recorded – but in 396 BCE the deadlock was broken in Rome's favour. Roman armies camped outside the city walls of Veii, while a tunnel was dug underneath them. The soldiers suddenly emerged from the tunnel inside a temple, and the combination of attacks both from within and without led to the fall of the city.

The second event was the fabled Gallic (Celtic) sack of Rome in 390 BCE. As with all of these early military encounters one of the casualties is the detail. A Gallic tribe under a resourceful leader, Brennus, searching for new land to settle, crossed the Alps and eventually forcefully entered Rome itself, where its citizens supposedly barricaded themselves on the Capitoline Hill. Humiliated, the Romans only managed to effect the withdrawal of the Gauls by paying a ransom of 1,000 pounds of gold. This incident of paying off the 'barbarians' would become an occasionally repeating theme in Rome's relationship with its enemies, both actual and potential, more so in the later empire. Harsh lessons had undoubtedly been learnt, however. The army was reformed and a new defensive wall, up to 10 m in height and 11 km long, was built to protect the city.

Intermittent warfare, perhaps campaigns every few years or so, gradually became an unofficial institution. The Romans fought at least three wars against the Samnites, a people of the central Apennines, between c. 350 and 300 BCE. There is another emerging theme here, one of martialism and returning heroes, the victors coming back in triumph with the spoils of war. Indeed the triumph (*triumphus*) was an official civil ceremony and religious rite of ancient Rome, held to celebrate publicly the achievement of an army commander who had won great military successes. In republican times, only the senate could grant a triumph, and one of the qualifications was that at least 5,000 enemy troops had to be killed. Soon the sight of returning victorious military leaders, laden with spoil, faces painted a spectacular scarlet, would become an eagerly expected event. It is easy to see how the city's inhabitants came to view successful military campaigns as essential to

Rome's wellbeing. An ideology of militarism coupled with a divine right of conquest, the success of which was displayed by bullion and treasure from sacked cities deposited in the temple treasuries and acknowledged by way of plentiful feasting for the masses, was a beguiling and addictive mix.

▶ Turning foes into friends

Why was Rome, as a city state, better at conquest than its equally aggressive neighbours in the Italian peninsula? After all, it was not unusual for societies to be overtly warlike and Rome did not enjoy any technological advantage. The answer may well lie in that uncanny ability that Rome had, especially in the republican period, to transform defeated enemies into loyal allies. It was a trick of statesmanship worth examining.

In the first centuries of Roman rule power over other peoples was exercised as a form of hegemony. Rome was able to dominate and control its neighbours, often after defeating them on the battlefield, by a form of overlordship that did not involve the exercise of direct control. During the fourth century BCE the Romans institutionalized these arrangements by developing and conferring a variety of statuses on the subordinate peoples, creating permanent obligations. Rome established itself as the pre-eminent city of Latium by granting 'Latin rights' to the inner circle of allied cities. With citizens of these places Rome's own citizens enjoyed certain reciprocal obligations. Beyond this inner ring was an outer group labelled *socii*, or allies. The Romans formed ties with communities, but inevitably these treaties were asymmetrical and created permanent subordination. Allied states had notional autonomy internally, but had to supply Rome with soldiers when requested, and had very little independence in terms of external relations. Above all, Roman hegemony was re-enforced through co-operation between elites of Rome and allied city states. This elaborate arrangement of treaties and rights between city states, coupled with elite links established by way of a one-sided patronage, formed a resilient and flexible network which would empower the Romans to become controllers of the entire Italian peninsula, and beyond.

▶ Into Africa: wars with Carthage

In the 150 or so years after c. 300 BCE Roman hegemony spread its web over the entire Mediterranean world. Viewed with hindsight it looks as if an overall strategy guided such impressive and rapid expansion, but in fact, although most individual military campaigns were highly organized, the end result of Mediterranean-wide control arose almost by accident. It took about 50 years for Roman influence to become a cause for concern for an empire on the North African coast: in this case Carthage. The cause of the conflict was geographically obvious: the large island of Sicily was a plum prize that stood between them. The first Punic war, fought mainly in naval engagements, ended in 241 BCE with Rome controlling

▲ The extent of Republican Rome's territories in 200 BCE, and an indication of the land controlled (darker shading) by its rival in North Africa, Carthage.

most of Sicily as its first overseas province. Now a naval power, Rome moved quickly to take over the islands of Corsica and Sardinia. The idea of extending hegemony overseas, outside the Italian peninsula, must have been alarming to some senators. It was not necessarily a given that Rome would seek out further conquests abroad.

The second Punic war must have heightened Rome's insecurities, perhaps persuading more of its politicians that its well being could only be guaranteed in the long term by extending its network territorially. Roman and Carthaginian interests clashed again in Spain, ultimately provoking the Carthaginian military commander, Hannibal, to launch an audacious strike against Italy by marching his men, including some elephants, across the Alps, where he negotiated alliances with some Celtic tribes of the Po valley. Initial victories over the Romans were achieved at the river Trebia (218 BCE), Trasimene (217 BCE) and Cannae (216 BCE) and even the fall of Rome seemed only a matter of time.

Yet Hannibal's campaign in southern Italy, although it lasted more than a decade in which he won over many of Rome's former allies, never conjured up the final assault on Rome. Roman armies, not daring to face the Carthaginian in an open, pitched battle, used scorched-earth tactics to make provisioning for the enemy difficult. Political factions in Carthage grew tired of the Italian campaign, and, deprived of reinforcements, Hannibal was recalled to North Africa to counter a Roman invasion army. The Roman general Scipio Africanus led this counter-offensive, having studied the military tactics of Hannibal carefully. A decisive battle was fought on African soil at Zama in 202 BCE resulting in the defeat of Hannibal and the imposition of a war indemnity on Carthage. Perhaps there is another significant reason here for Rome's supremacy: the ability to learn from others, particularly in terms of warfare. Allied to its policy of usually employing the troops of its allies, Rome's generals must have been open and willing to learn from a variety of military tactics they encountered in battle.

▶ Romans in Greece and the East

In 200 BCE a pivotal campaign took place against Philip II of Macedon, from which it is possible to get some insight into the debates in the senate and among the Roman populace that ultimately guided Rome's conquests. The reasons for Rome's intervention are unclear, but it may be that a pretext was sought in the treaty that Philip had made with Hannibal, when the latter was still a threat to Rome. The first time the Roman assembly was asked to approve the war, it refused to ratify the decision of the senate. That decision was rapidly reversed and we simply do not know what pressure or persuasion was placed on the citizen body to change its collective mindset. Were they reminded of the largesse that could come their way after a successful campaign and a distribution of the spoils of war? Or were they pressured by the increasingly competitive elite families of Rome anxious to secure a prestigious command for one of their own? The war was won in just three years but what followed then cast Rome in a new light. Sure enough a large indemnity was forced on Philip, and he had to surrender most of his fleet, along with a number of hostages including his son Demetrius, as a safeguard for the king's future good conduct. But at the Panhellenic Games at Corinth in 196 BCE the victorious Roman general Flamininus declared the freedom of the Greeks.

> *The Senate of Rome ... leaves the following states free, without garrisons, subject to no tribute, and in full enjoyment of their ancestral laws: the peoples of Corinth, Phocis, Locri...*

(*Polybius*, The Histories, *18.46.5*)

Rome was not, after all, intent on territorial annexation (at least not in the East) but cast itself in the role of liberator. Such intentions owed much to the norms of Hellenistic history and diplomacy and to the high regard Rome had for all things Greek. And indeed Rome was true to its word; in 194 BCE the Roman armies were withdrawn.

During this period the Romans seem ambivalent, unsure of whether to take the road that would lead to the direct acquisition of more lands. Roman armies campaigned in Anatolia (modern Turkey) but were also easily diverted to skirmishes in north Italy and Spain. The wars were immensely profitable, bringing treasures exhibited by triumphant generals to the citizens of Rome. It was as if the booty on offer was more than enough of a prize, and the hard task of controlling and administering more overseas possessions could be deferred, perhaps indefinitely. But eventually the celebrating had to give way to some harsher political objectives. Defeated foes could regroup, become stronger and threaten in the future. The destruction of both Corinth and Carthage grew inevitable. Rome was no longer always content to win and withdraw, extract booty and conclude asymmetrical treaties.

The Achaean League, a confederation of city states in the Peloponnese, fatally challenged Roman hegemony in 146 BCE. The Roman consul Mummius advanced with an army into the Peloponnese. The Achaean general Diaeus was camped at Corinth. After a battle in which the Romans suffered significant losses, the Achaeans were defeated, some fleeing to find refuge in Corinth. Roman revenge was immediate and violent: the city was utterly destroyed and all of its treasures and art shipped back to Rome.

> *I was there; I saw paintings trampled underfoot; soldiers sat down on them to play dice!*

(*Polybius*, The Histories, *39.2*)

The annihilation of Corinth marked an abrupt departure from previous Roman policy in Greece. In the same year Carthage, Rome's great rival in North Africa, was razed to the ground. This particular conflict – the third Punic war – had begun in 149 BCE, after successive Roman embassies had returned to Rome conveying anxieties about the ambitions of its old foe. In truth, it presented no real threat but the 'hawks' in the senate, including Senator Cato the Elder, urged a pre-emptive strike against Carthage before it became any stronger, or challenged Rome's trade networks . He was infamously fond of repeating his mantra at the end of his speeches, even if Carthage was not the main subject:

> *Carthago delenda est – Carthage must be destroyed*

(*Plutarch*, Life of Cato the Elder, *p.27*).

Cato eventually got his way; possibly his fellow senators thought that was the only way to silence him. To provoke a conflict the senate issued Carthage with an impossible ultimatum, requiring the citizens to move their city inland. The Greek author Polybius travelled with Scipio Africanus and observed the siege and eventual destruction of the North African city. Accounts of this event by nineteenth-century historians claimed that the Romans buried the city's rubble and ploughed it over, sowing salt into the soil. While this is no doubt a much later fabrication the story does evoke the Romans' increased tenacity and ruthlessness.

But even in mid-second century BCE opinions must have been divided in the senate as to the extent and direction of Rome's aspirations overseas. The Romans had no imperial model to follow, no clarified foreign

▲ An imagined depiction of Rome's final assault on Carthage. It brought a brutal end to Rome's wars with the Punic Empire

policy, but it seems that, following the destruction of Carthage and Corinth, Rome had begun to think of its hegemony in a slightly different light. Its network of alliances and treaties, and its sharing of differing grades of citizenship and rights to indigenous elites must have meant that as this network grew, so did the numbers of embassies arriving in Rome with entreaties to intercede in this or that dispute. The form of subordination that Rome exercised, and its ability to resolve issues through force of arms if necessary, meant that at some point the hegemonic process itself, its stresses and strains, provided the momentum for the expansion of influence. Basically, the dynamic favoured intervention; refusing to get involved was always much harder. Take the case of Attalus III, who died in 133 BCE leaving his kingdom of Pergamon to Rome in his will. Many Romans still had a reluctance to approve of acquisitions east of the Adriatic, and it was only when the popular assembly was promised that the proceeds of acquisition would be used to fund land distributions to the Italian poor that assent was given.

This evolving system of piecemeal control stretched and finally broke during the last century and a half of the republic. After accepting, albeit with some misgivings, the kingdom of Pergamon, Rome was still a power geared to arbitrary expansion, not a bureaucratic colonial power organised to tax provincials in an accountable manner. It preferred indirect rule through friendly client kings as opposed to direct control. The interventions in the East by Rome were not guided by any logical application of consistent foreign policy and were therefore unpredictable; no doubt they reflected the ever-changing politics and alliances of the senate, the assemblies and the elite families. Geography played its part too, as in Africa, the Middle East, Gaul, Spain and the Balkans the rule of Rome was deliberately restricted to the coastal fringes which offered familiar environments. The forests and mountains of the interior, though linked to the lowlands, were feared. As a policy this was bound to fail in the long run.

▶ The failure of republican government

A taste of the anarchy to come was provided at the turn of the first century BCE. Wars against the Celts in Gaul, Spain and Italy meant that Marius, one of the consuls, was elected an unprecedented seven times (the normal term was a single year only) to lead armies against the enemies of Rome. The Romans came under pressure from all sides, and on all sides there were opportunists ready to take a chance, both on land and sea. From 91 to 87 BCE Rome's allies in Italy rose in rebellion, eventually to be defeated but with the concession of Roman citizenship. In 102 BCE Antonius, a praetor, was given command against the pirates of the Mediterranean, who had clearly become a significant problem, presumably disrupting trading links, and carried it with such distinction that he was awarded a naval triumph. In 89 BCE Mithridates VI, King of Pontus (near the Black Sea), followed up a military victory over the Romans with a massacre of Roman and Italian settlers remaining in several Anatolian cities. Essentially this wiped out the Roman presence in the region, although he was eventually defeated and the *status quo* restored.

The last 60 years or so of the Roman republic ripped apart the delicate balances between official political authority, elite family competitiveness, military commands and the demands of Rome's masses that had steered the rise and expansion of Rome. Consuls, the leading magistrates elected by the popular assemblies, held onto military power, and were away from Rome, and independent of its control, for longer and longer periods. The potential was there for armed might to take precedence over centralised, political direction. Rome became mercy to the ambitions of successful rival generals and their loyal armies. Civil wars were the inevitable consequences.

It is clear, with hindsight, that the republican institutions that had fuelled Roman expansion were failing. Those mechanisms that had controlled a city state, or alliances of small kingdoms, were not sufficient to manage what in effect had become a vast empire. While political in-fighting escalated in Rome, her armies were responsible for the most dramatic phase of Roman expansion. On the slightest pretext generals in receipt of extraordinary commands marched to the shores of the Atlantic and Caspian Sea, deep into the forests of Europe and eastwards to confront the mighty Parthians.

The details, gripping though they are, can only be summarized here. In 60 BCE three wealthy senators and generals – Pompey, Crassus and Caesar – formed an unofficial alliance (a triumvirate) to co-ordinate political strategy. It proved effective for several years but the equilibrium was broken by the catastrophic defeat and death of Crassus in Syria in 53 BCE, along with the annihilation of 20,000 Romans, and the capture of another 10,000. For much of the 50s BCE Caesar campaigned in Gaul, eventually annexing most of the region. The families of Caesar and Pompey were linked through marriage (Pompey having married Julia, Caesar's daughter) but the death of the latter in childbirth heralded a new phase of friction between the two men. Events came to a head and in 49 BCE Caesar, with an army, famously crossed the Rubicon – a small river in north-east Italy that formed the frontier of his province – intending to challenge his rival. It did not go well for Pompey: he was defeated in battle and eventually hunted down to Egypt, where he was stabbed to death as he set foot on shore. Caesar became something that republicans were wary of: a Dictator. The office of Dictator was recognised but was only used in emergencies and for a six-month period. Caesar assumed it for ten years in 46 BCE and for life in 44 BCE.

Caesar did not enjoy his autocracy for very long. Many senators considered that Caesar was attempting to become a king, and plotted to kill him.

The conspirators never met exactly openly, but they assembled a few at a time in each other's homes ... Someone proposed that they draw lots for some to

▲ The assassination of Julius Caesar, an event that would eventually lead to the inauguration of the first Emperor, Augustus.

push him from the bridge and others to run up and kill him. A third plan was to wait for a coming gladiatorial show. The advantage of that was, because of the show, no suspicion would be aroused if arms were seen

(Nicolaus of Damascus, Life of Augustus, p.23).

In 44 BCE, as a result of this conspiracy led by Brutus and Cassius and involving about 60 senators, Caesar was stabbed to death on the Ides (15th) of March near the Theatre of Pompey or the Senate House (according to which ancient author you believe). Caesar's most celebrated last words *'Et tu, Brute?'* were in fact an invention of Shakespeare in his play *Julius Caesar* (1599).

In the turmoil that followed some coherence was achieved through another alliance of three great men – Mark Antony, Lepidus and Octavian – in 43 BCE. Octavian, (later Emperor Augustus), was Caesar's great nephew, and adopted son and heir. This second triumvirate lost no time in dealing with its enemies, both at home and abroad. Cicero, an influential protagonist of the republic, was hunted down and beheaded. His head and both his hands (which had penned texts against Mark Antony) were displayed in the forum at Rome, while Mark Antony's wife, Fulvia, cut out his tongue and repeatedly pierced it with her hairpin in a final act of retribution against the great orator's powers of speech. Brutus and Cassius, the so-called 'Liberators', were defeated in two battles at Philippi in Macedonia by Octavian and Mark Anthony.

▶ The birth of empire

Power-sharing didn't provide stability, however. Octavian eventually quarrelled with Lepidus in 36 BCE, accusing him of plotting rebellion in Sicily. Lepidus got off lightly. He was exiled to a small coastal town south of Rome where he lived peacefully for over 20 years. Mark Antony was not so lucky. He was infatuated by Cleopatra, seriously compromising his loyalties, and the Roman senate declared war on Egypt. Octavian won the naval battle of Actium, near the Gulf of Corinth, in 31 BCE; Alexandria was then besieged until Mark Antony and Cleopatra committed suicide. Octavian now became the most powerful man in the Roman world. The senate bestowed the title of Augustus on him in

▲ Bust of the Emperor Augustus in Trier Museum. The wreath of oak or Civic Crown was granted to the young Emperor by the Senate.

27 BCE, and although Augustus was careful to defer to the authority of the senate, often dissembling his absolute power, Rome gradually came to realise that the republic was dead. It now had its first emperor: *Imperator*, an ancient title but one now used to signify absolute authority.

It was not only the republic that was over. The Romans' use of hegemony and indirect control was gradually transformed into more direct rule under a truly imperial ideology. The first two centuries of the Roman empire proper were still punctuated by episodes of expansionary conquest, by occasional defeats, by 'bad' emperors and by civil wars, but the imperial system held fast. The adventurous campaigns of Roman armies in far-flung lands gave way to concerns based around security, defence, and the better organization of the territories controlled by Rome. Augustus opened the imperial history of Rome with a period of expansion and territorial 'tidying up', including completing the conquest of Spain.

> I extended the territory of all those provinces of the Roman people on whose borders lay peoples not subject to our government

(Augustus, Res Gestae, 26.1).

But there were reverses. Augustus's campaigns in northern Europe, and particularly his designs on lands east of the Rhine, were halted by the defeat of Roman general Varus and the extermination of three legions in 9 CE, at the hands of Arminius. Transition from one emperor to another, always a moment of supreme political tension, showed that the messy process could survive the occasional imperial assassination. After the assassination of Caligula there was a brief attempt by conspirators to restore the republic, but the Praetorian Guard (effectively the emperor's personal bodyguards) commandeered Caligula's uncle, Claudius, pushing him into power. Claudius himself was subsequently responsible for the invasion of Britain and the addition of a new province to the empire.

The emperors, as an institution, also demonstrated that they could survive civil wars (or at least one of them could) when Vespasian emerged triumphant from the so-called 'year of four emperors', 69 CE. This was significant for it now clearly underlined that imperial authority rested on control of the armies. There were further campaigns of territorial expansion, although tellingly some of these were prompted by attacks on the Roman frontier, and by the need for plunder to subsidise the massive expenditure required by the Roman treasury, much of it spent on the army. In the winter of 85–86 CE the army of King Duras of Dacia attacked the Roman province of Moesia, crossing the Danube and killing the governor, Oppius Sabinus, a former consul. It was to take 20 years and two campaigns before Emperor Trajan was able to raze the Dacian capital, Sarmizegethusa, to the ground and create a new Roman province. The events were recorded on Trajan's Column in Rome. In 106 CE Arabia was annexed and Trajan's Parthian conquests took the Roman Empire to its greatest territorial extent. His successor Hadrian was more conservative, constructing during his reign the eponymous wall across the north of England, and withdrawing from the new province of Mesopotamia.

▶ Stretched to breaking point

The high-water mark of empire had been reached and the ebb tide imperceptibly tugged at its imperial frontiers. In the 160s CE the empire's eastern and northern edges were weakened through wars with Parthia, the import of plague by means of returning soldiers, and the movements of tribes across its north-eastern frontier. The 170s and 180s CE saw Germanic and north European tribal incursions across the Danube, (some of which managed to penetrate as far as northern Italy), the lengthy absence of Emperor Marcus Aurelius from Rome to contain them, and an eventual peace treaty signed with two tribes, the Marcomanni and the Quadi. But the empire was slowly transforming into something more cosmopolitan than Augustus could have dreamt of. Septimius Severus, emperor from 193 to 211 CE, was of African descent, Caracalla granted universal Roman citizenship in 212 CE, and one of Septimius's successors, Elagabalus, was born in Emesa in present-day Syria. If there is a single period when the slow but uneven decline of Rome can first be marked, then the 230s CE, the end of the Severan dynasty, has a better claim than most other decades.

Looking back on Rome's appetite for warfare and subsequent conquests over a period of 600 years or so, it seems clear that the scale, frequency and length of Roman warfare, its ability to suffer considerable losses, its capacity for sustained violence and its ability to learn from the tactics of others were unusual in the pre-modern period. But what is also demonstrable is that there was no overall guiding strategy; there was rather a repeated expediency driven by the dynamics of elite familial competitiveness, the politics of Rome, the masses, the legions, the lust for booty and ambitious military commanders. Such a cocktail of influences meant that Roman hegemony and then empire constantly evolved, changing character, and was often beyond the control of any particular group of people or indeed individual. Different decades could be dominated by different Romans who favoured different forms of Roman rule. It is time to take a closer look at the way Rome ruled and the instruments of its control.

The rulers of Rome

The nature of Roman rule clearly changed considerably over the 1,000 years or more of the Roman republic and empire. The Romans needed mechanisms to debate and discuss issues, promulgate laws, and enforce and police them, as well as the not inconsiderable task of keeping the actual peace – the fabled *pax romana* – throughout the territories that Rome controlled. We can begin by looking at the political machinery in Rome itself: the senate and its magistrates and the assemblies of the citizen body. This will lead to an examination of the role of the governors of the provinces, who were usually senators and ex-magistrates themselves. The political functions of the cities were vitally important, as were the sympathies of the local elites of the indigenous populations. In the imperial period the wishes of the emperor were almost, but not quite, paramount.

A straightforward description of the components of imperial rule can easily disguise how long it actually took for decisions at the top to work through the system. A quick and effective change in any aspect of law or administration was almost impossible. The slowness of communications between centre and periphery and the limited manpower for supervising and enforcing unpopular changes over the vast area of the empire meant that things could only change gradually and, in the face of opposition from some of the government's own personnel, perhaps not at all. A significant component of government was the army, whose composition and duties changed as the republic fell into the early empire, and the latter metamorphosed into late empire.

▶ At the centre of the Earth

The Greek observer Polybius labelled republican government at Rome a 'mixed constitution' and described it as an unique balance of monarchical, aristocratic and democratic elements, as represented by the magistrates, the senators and the assemblies of the people. We can take a look at how these functioned in the first half of the second century BCE. The most senior magistrates were the two consuls. They could take charge of armies, they could uphold jurisdiction, they could issue instructions in the form of edicts, and they could propose legislation to the assemblies. When one or both were in Rome it was normally a consul who controlled the deliberations of the senate. There were limits to their power, however: they were elected officials, their office was limited to one year only and early re-election was not permitted. Other magistrates included praetors (four to six in number) who dealt with legal matters, quaestors (eight) who supervised financial matters, aediles (four) who were responsible for public festivals, censors (two) responsible for registration of citizens and the expenditure on public buildings, and tribunes (ten) who represented the views of the citizen body.

All magistrates were theoretically elected for a single year by the citizen body, although elections were weighted in favour of the wealthier classes, and the poorest citizens might not be called upon to vote. The citizen body was also responsible for approving all important decisions, such as a declaration of war. The senate, which numbered approximately 300 senators enrolled for life, was in theory only an advisory body, but in practice it issued instructions such as where armies were to be deployed, and it received and responded to the increasing number of foreign embassies who petitioned the Romans.

The senate was dominated by ancient elite families, a large proportion of consuls and praetors being descended from former magistrates. It was not, therefore, divided by fairly rigid political philosophies as are most contemporary Western democracies, but by inter-family competitions for honour (especially of the military kind), status and wealth. But the constraints of senatorial office, and how they could be overcome, were occasionally apparent. Already some magistrates had seized the opportunity for military commands of extraordinary length to enhance the standing of their families. Scipio Africanus, victor over Hannibal, had campaigned at the head of his army for almost ten years, returning to Rome, still an ambitious young man, to host a fabulous triumph. In addition, from time to time, it was possible for energetic political leaders to appeal directly to the people, especially through bribes and gifts. These developments found full and destructive expression in the civil wars of the following century.

If political power in Rome was effected by successfully negotiating the balance between magistracy, the senate and the popular assemblies, in contrast the role of governor of a province was less restrained by such considerations. Governors were recruited from among the ex-consuls and ex-praetors; they were known as proconsuls or propraetors and usually served for two to three years in a particular province. A key duty of the governor was to command the army in his territory, although many had no formal military training. One of the most important officials on the staff of any governor was the quaestor. Elected by the people and assigned to a particular province by lot, the quaestor was in charge of provincial finances, and was often assigned other administrative duties. Thus Cicero, who was governor of Cilicia (part of southern Turkey) in 50 BCE, left his quaestor in charge of the province when he returned to Rome, even though he admitted that he was

a mere boy and probably stupid, frivolous and incapable of self-restraint

(*Cicero*, Letters to Atticus, *VI 6.3*).

Other officials on the governor's staff included *legati*, who were effectively deputies chosen for their specialist skills, *praefecti* who were minor military commanders, and *apparitores*, who functioned like civil servants. The last group of staff taken by the governor were the *comites*, young men who were personal friends or relations and who were keen to experience provincial administration.

Provincial governors often found themselves in charge of thousands of battle-hardened troops, and the latter must have viewed some governors as completely out of their depth. Again the example of Cicero is instructive. He found himself in charge of two legions, which if at full strength would equate to approximately 10,000 men. He was aged 55 and his last military experience had been as an 18 year old. He contented himself with capturing bandit strongholds, hoping that this might even earn him a triumph back in Rome. He was to be disappointed. Tackling bandits must have been significant to Cicero, since earlier he had famously prosecuted Verres, the ex-governor of Sicily, berating him for allowing pirates to maraud in the Great Harbour of Syracuse.

> *In the very harbour of Syracuse a pirate ship celebrated a triumph over the fleet of the Roman people, while its oars splashed water into the eyes of that shiftless and worthless Governor*
>
> (*Cicero*, Verres 2, *5.100*).

The other major duty falling to the governor was the upholding of provincial law. The governor had to adjudicate on a large number of legal conflicts and had the power to punish anyone, apart from Roman citizens, with flogging, death or large-scale confiscation of property. Cicero delighted in the freedom of his legal authority, with no public assemblies or complaints procedure to hold him to account. By contrast, in the reign of Trajan, the Younger Pliny, as governor of Bithynia, referred many matters to the imperial exchequer for clarification or advice (Pliny, *Letters*, 10).

▶ At the centre of the universe

When Rome became an imperial power, the balanced 'mixed constitution' lost its equilibrium. Octavian, later

Augustus, the first emperor of Rome, gradually transformed himself from deferent ruler, *primus inter pares*, to someone of quasi-divine status. He did so by delicately massaging the egos of senators, some of whom were just looking for an opportunity to restore the republic. In January 27 BCE Octavian was granted the title of Augustus, a vast province (half the Empire) for ten years and the right to rule through *legati* (deputies). But in 23 BCE he resigned the last of a series of consulships and was then granted in return a supreme command that allowed him, in effect, to outrank any governor in his province. Augustus also passed his legislation through the senate, appointing senators to almost all the major military and political commands, and reserving the right to veto appointments to others. In such a fashion, although his successors came to be referred to as 'Emperor', he cleverly accumulated vast wealth and power, without creating any new constitutional position. The veiled threat of military force underlined his authority. The senate still functioned, and senators could still convince themselves they were the collective decision-making body in Rome, but in essence the balance of power, disguised though it was, was wielded by one man.

Augustus – the paramount Roman for an astonishing 45 years – died in 14 CE at Nola, in Campania. Nothing emphasized more the transition wrought under him than his death and subsequent funeral. Among his last public words were the declaration:

I found Rome a city of bricks; I leave it to you as a city of marble

(*Cassius Dio*, Roman History, *56.30.3*).

The will that Augustus had left with the priestesses of Vesta was astonishing in its scale and reach. He included legacies to every Roman citizen and every soldier in the army. The will was supplemented by three codicils. The first was essentially an end-of-reign statement of accounts for the empire, detailing what soldiers were stationed where, how much money was in the treasuries, and the names of slaves and ex-slaves who held further details. This document appears to demonstrate that Augustus managed the accounts for the empire largely through his personal household, and not through the usual magistracies of the senate.

The second codicil included the instructions for his funeral: cremation from a tower-like pyre erected on the Campus Martius. An eagle would be released from the tower the moment the pyre was ignited, carrying his soul with it. He would be deified, like Julius Caesar, his great-uncle. The third codicil known as the Achievements of the Deified Augustus – *Res Gestae Divi Augusti* – gave an account of his life, to be inscribed on tablets and set up all over the empire. The best surviving example comes from a temple of the imperial cult at Ankara (Turkey). The heading in Greek reads:

Translated and inscribed below are the deeds and gifts of the god Augustus, the account of which he left in the city of Rome engraved on two bronze tablets

(*Augustus*, Res Gestae).

It is difficult to contemplate a more lasting testament to the first emperor of Rome. Through his conquests, gifts, and monuments he seems benefactor, conqueror (with a much more personal relationship to his key military officers), administrator and protector, and ultimately god, all rolled into one. Hegemonic overlordship had finally given way to direct territorial rule. Government at the centre was now an autocratic iron fist concealed in a pseudo-republican glove. Successive emperors would attempt to match his legacy; most would fail.

One who perhaps does stand comparison is Hadrian, emperor from 117 CE until his death in 138 CE. He came to power at a time when the empire was dangerously overstretched, particularly in the Middle East. He dedicated himself to stabilizing the territories that Rome controlled, personally criss-crossing the empire in two long journeys that would keep him away from Rome for almost half of his reign. Government business was carried out wherever he was, and embassies and delegations had to find him, not go to Rome.

Hadrian, compared with his aggressive predecessor Trajan, comes across as a far-sighted peacemaker, who launched no wars of conquest. Indeed one of his first actions was to withdraw the Roman army from Mesopotamia – present-day Iraq – an act that has a particular resonance for early twenty-first-century politics. One of the most celebrated monuments associated with Hadrian was the construction of his fortified wall, a barrier between present-day north of England and the Scottish borderlands. This is a monument that reflects a military ideology of consolidation, marking a limit to Roman rule, and calling a halt to any expansionist projects.

As a person Hadrian was passionately interested in Greek culture, shown not least in his close relationship with a Greek companion Antinous. He revitalized the Greek-speaking territories within the Empire and laid the foundations for the transformation of the Roman Empire into its Byzantine successor centuries later. Like Augustus he also added significantly to the architectural grandeur of Rome, ordering the reconstruction of the Pantheon, and his own Mausoleum, now the famous landmark of Castel Sant'Angelo. Hadrian was deified shortly after his death and gold coins commemorated his transformation, showing him being carried to the heavens by a mighty eagle.

However, there were many incompetent and corrupt emperors, some caricatured by classical authors, thus ensuring that their infamy continues to provide voyeuristic entertainment today. Imperial character assassinations stem from the lascivious anecdotes penned by authors such as Suetonius, who once served Hadrian. Emperor Nero, who committed suicide at the age of 31, was vilified again and again.

Whenever he floated down the Tiber to Ostia, or cruised past the Gulf of Baiae, he had a row of temporary brothels erected along the shore, where married

▲ The interior of the Pantheon in Rome, with light streaming in from the heavens through the oculus in the roof.

women, pretending to be inn-keepers,
solicited him to come ashore

(*Suetonius*, The Twelve Caesars, *VI, 27*).

At some dinner parties he hosted, Nero invited dancing girls and prostitutes from all over Rome. He forced his friends to be equally lavish, making one of them spend 40,000 gold pieces on a 'turban party'.

▶ WMD? – The Roman army

Rome conquered new territories, enforced peace, put down rebellions and kept the 'barbarians' at bay by use of its formidable armies, made up of Roman citizen soldiers and auxiliaries supplied by allies. Without the legions there would have been no empire. What made the Roman army a seemingly unstoppable force?

The army of the early republic predominantly consisted of warriors called hoplites, foot-soldiers heavily armed with spear, helmet, greaves, breastplate and a round shield. They fought in close formation called a phalanx, and both armour and formation were adopted from the Greeks, particularly through contact with early Greek colonies in southern Italy and Sicily. These organised systems gradually emerged from earlier styles of confrontations, fought in a quasi-heroic fashion by aristocrats and their kinsmen. The hoplites were usually wealthy landowners who could afford the weaponry, and they returned to their homes after the fighting ceased.

The phalanx had probably been discarded by the mid-fourth century BCE and we are lucky that we have a detailed description of the new arrangements by a second-century BCE eyewitness, the Greek historian Polybius. A full consular army now consisted of two legions, each comprising 4,200 infantry and 300 cavalry. The basic tactical unit of the legion was the *maniple*, composed of 120 men divided into two 'centuries', each with its own centurion, standard-bearer and *optio*, the second-in-command. Marching camps – temporary camps to house the troops when on the march – became standardized in layout. The Roman army of the republic, however, remained a temporary citizen-militia. To spread the burden of military service no man was obliged to serve in more than 16 campaigns or years. Additional weapons now included a sword, probably adopted from a type the Romans had encountered in Spain, and chain-mail armour, cavalry harnesses and saddles, which the Romans copied from the Gauls. Herein lies one of the secrets of Rome's military prowess: the ability to learn from their opponents and absorb enemy tactics and weapons and make them their own. A spectacular example of this characteristic concerns the development of the Roman navy. Romans learnt how to build warships and engage in naval battles from hard lessons learned during their wars with Carthage, when initially the African city possessed much more sophisticated ships.

Towards the end of the second century BCE the continued expansion of the territories controlled by Rome meant that a part-time citizen militia could no longer hope to keep peace on the frontiers. A series of reforms to the military structure began which culminated in the creation of a fully professional army under the first emperors. Military service now became a career which lasted for much of a man's life, so that soldiers became increasingly separated from civilians. Legionaries were no longer men of property, which meant they had no source of livelihood after service. They were often granted monies and land when their military careers were over, frequently choosing to settle in provinces where they had served. Inevitably career soldiers developed fierce loyalties towards their commanders. Their commanders provided them opportunities for plunder, and they in turn could be persuaded by unscrupulous generals to shift their loyalty from the state to a military patron and fight his rivals in civil wars.

The professional legion consisted of ten cohorts deployed in three lines when in battle formation. Each cohort comprised six centuries of 80 men each, so a legion contained about 4,800 men. On average the

▲ The extent of the Empire early in the 1st century CE. Note that Britain was not annexed until 43 CE.

army numbered about 30 legions during the first three centuries of the empire, a relatively small force for such an extensive empire. Weaponry had evolved too, and now included metal segmented protection for the upper body of a legionary soldier, two throwing spears, a short cut-and-thrust sword called a *gladius*, and the more familiar *scutum*, a large rectangular shield behind which a man could crouch down for protection. A legionary soldier was not allowed to marry, although in practice many formed liaisons with local women where they served. The allied forces, the *auxilia*, who often fought under their own tribal commanders, also became more professional, supplying cavalry, archers and slingers. In the early empire auxiliary soldiers retired after 25 years of service, at which time they were awarded Roman citizenship. Actual combat only amounted to a minority of a soldier's time in service; in times of peace soldiers had other roles, for example as administrators, surveyors or builders, or in policing and in industries such as mining.

In the later empire, the third and fourth centuries CE, Roman provinces were increasingly challenged from within by civil wars, and from without by external invasions. These changing circumstances transformed the army, as defence of fortified positions became more important, and speed of movement was put at a premium. The differences between legionaries and *auxilia* dwindled, as a new distinction emerged: that between field armies and static frontier troops. The size of legions also shrank dramatically, down to probably no more than 1,000 men. However, as the warlike character of the imperial populations everywhere was blunted by generations of peace, significant numbers of recruits now needed to be drawn from communities of 'barbarian' tribes who had been allowed to settle within the empire, and this probably increased the overall numbers, perhaps swelling the number of soldiers in the Roman armies to over 500,000. Military weapons and dress had changed considerably. Shields were now oval in shape, and by the fourth century infantry and cavalry were equipped with a long-bladed sword worn on the left side. Trousers too became the norm; clothing once seen as typically 'barbarian'.

In summary, the Roman army, its organization, strength, weaponry, tactics and recruits, metamorphosed gradually, in relation to changing political circumstances and direction, the enemies it encountered and the growth of Roman territory. The flexibility it displayed, allied to its formidable discipline, an unswerving execution of violence and resolute vengeance gave it supremacy in the ancient world. The words of Polybius make that plain enough:

So you can often see in cities captured by the Romans not only people who have been butchered, but even dogs hacked in two, and the limbs of other animals cut off

(Polybius, The Histories, *10.15.4-5*).

▶ Rule from the cities

In the Roman world cities were the main centres of life and the administrative hubs through which local government was effected. Rome organized its relationships to cities by treaty, with agreements for cooperation or the imposition of terms after opposition or defeat. Generally speaking each city controlled a rural hinterland. Each city was also formally and distinctively constituted, with certain civic rights and obligations for its residents, and a code of laws and institutions through which civic affairs were managed, in theory by the adult male citizens. Rome, after all, was a city state in origin, ruled by magistracies, the senate and assemblies of the people. This was the model that Rome encouraged in the provinces. Occasionally Rome supplemented indigenous cities by founding new ones with land allotments for colonists, many of whom could be retired soldiers. However, some 'colonies' involved the promotion of cities of mainly non-Roman people with the co-operation of local elites.

The formality of the system produced a sort of league table of the status of different cities. At the top were Roman citizen colonies (*coloniae*), which could be exempt from taxation. Then there were municipal cities (*municipia*) where all citizens enjoyed the benefits of Roman citizenship. Lesser municipalities with 'Latin rights' occurred in which citizenship was restricted to just the members of the governing council, or, more strictly, to its ex-magistrates. Finally there was the indigenous city, of so-called 'peregrine' status; there the residents preserved their own laws and customs, although Roman citizens could live among them.

The standard institutions of city government throughout the empire were annual magistracies and councils. Magistrates were elected by an assembly of adult male citizens, which could also be called on to vote on other matters previously discussed by the council. The names of these magistracies, their duties and the relationship between the institutional components of local government, could vary from city to city. As such the city government could be either oligarchical (generally favoured by the Roman authorities) or democratic, or any shade in between. Membership of a council was normally hereditary and numbers varied between East and West. In the former a council could consist of as many as 450 members, while in the latter, 100 or fewer was probably the norm. In any decision-making body of those sizes factions frequently formed and disagreements broke out. Assemblies of citizens had a role to play, even if our ancient sources are not precise on their exact contribution. Formal votes to endorse a decision of the council could be taken by a properly constituted citizen assembly, but it could equally make its views known by cheers, chanting of slogans, or by hisses and jeers in an informal gathering in the forum or theatre.

At the town (*municipium*) of Irni, in Spain, where the minimum number of councillors was 63, a list of a magistrates' duties has survived. The aediles at Irni had a variety of duties which included the right to administer the corn supply, the sacred buildings and holy places, the roads, the district, the drains, the baths, the market, the inspection of weights and measures and the city watch, which was probably concerned principally with fire-fighting. Local magistrates also had some part to play in policing, which entailed vigorously pursuing runaway slaves and stolen animals. Nevertheless citizens often found it more useful to appeal to the gods than the local authorities, as this curse tablet from Uley in Gloucestershire, illustrates:

Memorandum to the god Mercury from Saturnina, woman, about linen goods which she has lost – that the thief, whether man or woman, slave or free, have no ease unless and until he brings the aforesaid goods to the aforesaid temple – and Saturnina promises Mercury a third part of the value of the property recovered

(Hassall and Tomlin, Britannia, *10, 1979, 343, no. 3*).

In passing, this curse is a good example of the very practical, transactional nature of everyday religious practices in the Roman empire.

The central government in Rome laid certain obligations on city governments, and failure to meet them would undoubtedly mean direct intervention; this certainly applied to the payment of direct taxes. Generally it was not wise for a city to do anything that might be construed as neglectful of Roman interests, nor should it allow repeated civic disorders. There must have been a delicate balance to maintain between a city, the provincial government and the emperor. Cities were keen to be seen as proactive in their loyalty, and often approached the governor or the emperor to seek permission for certain schemes, many associated with the imperial cult.

Already by the second century CE enthusiasm for civic office among the provincial wealthy was on the wane, not least because of the time involved in performing all the necessary duties and the cost of making the expected financial contributions to public buildings. A second-century CE inscription from Nîmes attests to loans advanced by a freedman to local magistrates in order for them to meet the expenses of their offices. By the fourth century CE civic office had lost its appeal completely and was therefore made compulsory.

One more aspect of civic administration must be mentioned: the status of women. Women could not become members of the council but the wealthy among them could hold offices as priestesses in the public cults of the city. At Aphrodisias (Turkey) there were both priests and priestesses of Aphrodite, and also a category of girls called 'flower-bearers'; these presumably carried flowers in processions for Aphrodite. Women could also make donations, but these were often in the name of a dead husband or of an infant son. They were occasionally rewarded with titles, such as 'Mother of the City', but these conferred no official status other than the name.

▶ Friendly kings and elites

At this juncture in our discussion of rulers it is useful to look at some numbers. We have noted that the empire was home to some 60 to 70 million people at its height in the early second century CE. The rulers we have identified so far were the senators, magistrates, governors and their agents, and the emperor and his imperial household. There was also the army and its allied troops. Altogether these probably amount to no more than 350,000 people in the early empire. The great majority of these were soldiers who, in the imperial period, were stationed at or near the frontiers, or on actual campaign. Without wanting to be too precise, it seems clear that Roman administrators were spread very thinly among the provincial populations. So how were law, order, and the all important collection of taxes maintained?

The answers to these questions are at least twofold. In the first instance, in a practice that went back to the early years of the republic, the Romans encouraged the local elites of neighbouring cities to appreciate the benefits of Roman citizenship and certain elements of the Roman 'cultural package'. Indeed some argue that, for the Romans, citizenship was a far more important concept than ethnicity. As we have seen, the senate could be dominated by successive generations of elite families. These families could in turn form particular links with wealthy or noble provincial families, who enjoyed citizenship, strengthened through patron-client relationships. At the highest level there were therefore familial and horizontal connections that cut across the dichotomy of Romans as conquerors and provincials as conquered. The encouragement of local elites to 'join the club' has been described as one of emulation or euergetism. A classic example is the flatteringly magnanimous picture that Tacitus paints of his father-in-law Agricola as governor of Britain.

His object was to accustom them to a life of peace and quiet by the provision of amenities. He therefore gave official assistance to the building of temples, public squares and good houses. He educated the sons of the chiefs in the liberal arts, and expressed a preference for British ability as compared to the trained skills of the Gauls. The result was that instead of loathing the Latin language they became eager to speak it effectively. In the same way, our national dress came into favour and the toga was everywhere to be seen. And so the population was gradually led into the demoralizing temptation of arcades, baths and sumptuous banquets. The unsuspecting Britons spoke of such novelties as 'civilization', when in fact they were only a feature of their enslavement

(*Tacitus*, Agricola, *21*).

This particular quote demonstrates the powerfully seductive effect of Roman culture, and especially material culture: the objects and public buildings that Romans took for granted. Notable is the tactic of educating the sons of local chiefs. Whether the Britons, or any other annexed provincials, were as 'unsuspecting' as Tacitus maintained is debateable.

In the second instance the Romans made frequent use of the concept of friendly kings (also known less accurately as client kings), particularly near the empire's borders. These kings were allowed to rule over their territories free from direct Roman interference in return for some concessions to Rome such as maintaining internal order, suppression of banditry and piracy, and the occasional contribution of soldiers to augment Rome's forces. There is no evidence that these monarchs were regarded as temporary and expedient rulers, to be replaced in the fullness of time by direct rule. When their territories were annexed it was usually a Roman response to a royal failure, not an anticipated strategic intervention. These kings varied widely in individual status, from Cleopatra of Egypt to Herod the Great of Judaea to Bocchus of Mauretania (Morocco) to Togidubnus of southern Britain. One public demonstration of Augustus's power was the number of kings who came to seek his protection. From their supplications the emperor gained much prestige. In return some kings proclaimed themselves 'Friend of Rome', sometimes on their coins as did Herod of Chalcis, a kingdom north of Judaea in present-day Lebanon.

It is not easy to summarize the position of these friendly kings, or their subjects, since by nature they varied enormously. If we take the example of Togidubnus of the Atrebates, he was probably elevated to kingship by the Romans in 43 CE, apparently ruling a large area of southern Britain nominally independent of Roman rule. Was he proud to be associated with Rome? Was he able to maintain some sort of dual identity, part Roman in public, mostly Atrebatic in private? Did he keep Roman officials at bay by a series of calculated concessions? And what of his elite circle of supporters, or further, the populace at large? Did the status of their friendly kingdom impinge on their lives at all? Easy questions to ask, but definitive answers are difficult.

Finally, efficient rule was, and is, dependent on the speed of communication. Messages across the empire travelled on horseback or by sea. Estimates vary as to how fast such means could be, and even with the truism that bad news travelled faster than good news, there must have been many instances of crucial messages taking weeks and months to arrive. Inevitably this could produce uncertainty or unwanted actions on the frontiers, and frustrated waiting in Rome on the outcome of events. A corollary of slow communications was the lack of any mass media; images on coins were the nearest thing the ancient world possessed. Getting at 'the truth' must have meant wading through waves of rumours. Ruling such a large empire must have been affected at times by the consequences of the delayed receipt of news and by collective belief in rumour.

The common people

Having looked at the way Rome imposed some sort of rule over its subjects, it is crucial that we turn the coin over to look at the reverse image: the masses of people, at least 60 million of them, who dwelt within Roman-controlled territories. By and large we hear much less of them. Sometimes they might feature in the accounts of classical authors, usually as a result of disturbances or revolts, sometimes as willing recipients of Roman culture. They are there to reflect the triumph of Roman 'civilized' life-styles. Archaeology provides some illumination – for instance the epitaphs on gravestones that might mention an indigenous tribal identity – but often the evidence is ambiguous and capable of multiple interpretations.

The political unification that the Romans imposed from Syria to Scotland did not result in anything like a homogeneous 'Roman society'. Indeed there must have been members of some rural communities who did not realise they were even in the Roman empire. Indeed, just what geo-political awareness would the average farm-worker or herdsman in the remote mountains of Galicia or on the edges of the Sahara have had of the Roman world? Their consciousness was not one informed by literacy, but by orally transmitted indigenous information. They had no maps showing imperial frontiers. They may not have even known that a new type of pottery vessel was 'Roman'. Their most obvious link to the wider and differently organized world may have been the unwelcome arrival of someone to collect an annual tribute, or a call to be registered by a census that took place at irregular intervals.

Roman rule was therefore exercised over a kaleidoscope of different societies, numbering hundreds and probably thousands. Indeed Rome may have created some of these communities through the act of military overlordship and the imposition of direct rule. Roman military and administrative leaders preferred to deal with societies that were equally hierarchically structured, and like other more recent colonial powers, where none existed, they sought to create communities or tribes by re-settlement or coercion of different groups to form a new unity, headed up by a leader or chief of some sort.

Despite the slowness and hazards of road and sea travel, some people did move around. Serving soldiers or those connected with the military were the most frequent category who found themselves away from home; sometimes a long way from home. There is a famous tombstone of the second century CE from South Shields (*Arbeia* or 'Arabs') that records the death of a Catuvellaunian wife commemorated by one Barates, who was probably a trader from Palmyra in present-day Syria. The epitaph is both in Latin and Palmyrene. A host of soldiers drawn from different ethnic groups served on this remote frontier: Tungrians (from Belgium), Dacians (Romania), Asturians (Spain), Batavians (Netherlands), Lingones (France) and most strikingly 'foreign' of all, boatmen from the Tigris (Iraq). But it was not only soldiers or auxiliaries that served in distant lands. Slaves were transported considerable distances, not least to lessen their chances of escaping back home. Estimates suggest that immigrants in Rome at the height of empire constituted at least five per cent of the city's population, while even in the early fifth century CE pilgrims, priests, families and children all journeyed far from their places of birth.

A crucial distinction in the Roman world was between the city and the countryside. 'Civilized' life could only be conducted in the cities, and in well-appointed country retreats, like villas, especially if their owners maintained a residence in the nearest town. The great majority of people who did not live in cities or towns were probably stigmatized as 'uncivilized barbarians'. Predominantly rural peoples or communities were conveniently stereotyped for the appreciation of the Roman elite.

According to Tacitus, the Germans were a barbaric people, characterized by the lack of developed agriculture and an emphasis on pastoralism. German men were idle, ate and drank a lot, and were prone to fighting; what little ploughing they did was the prerogative of their women. Their ideals were completely opposite to those espoused by the Romans. They had no cities and counted time by nights, not by days, leading to a loss of the sense of chronological order. Bad reputations were not confined to the West: in Anatolia the Mysians, Phrygians and Carians were commonly despised as slavish and cowardly; Syrian Jews and Idumeans were looked on as bold schemers, Phoenicians as addicted to astrology and Arabs as born liars, prone to huckstering. The attitudes of Roman provincial administrators to such peoples when trouble arose included punitive interventions and subsequent enslavements of some of the population, or a laissez-faire attitude in times of peace when taxes or tribute were paid, or deliberate encouragement of the Roman way of life. The last attitude was immortalised, albeit with a chilling irony, by Tacitus when he described the laudable efforts of Agricola, the governor of Britain (see quotation cited at the end of Chapter 3).

The question of identity, therefore, amongst the massed communities ruled by the Romans was a complex one. For most of the millions, whose rural lives were based in agriculture, their 'identity' cannot have been of much conscious significance, but their allegiance must have been to the community (or people, tribe or region) in which they grew up, whether an artificial entity manufactured by foreign administrators or not. For dwellers in towns or cities they no doubt felt they were bound to a particular urban settlement. Identity could be a multiple phenomenon. You could be defined by your occupation, by gender, by your status as freeborn, freedman or slave, or by your worship of a particular cult and still be an inhabitant of a specific city or region. You could juggle, conceal or present your identities as circumstances encouraged. The Roman empire was characterized by racial stereotyping, ethnic divides and numerous prejudices, resulting in criss-crossing fault lines, some of which any particular tension could bring into play. In the lands ruled by Rome, there was no satisfaction in a multi-cultural empire, no melting-pot, no senatorial opprobrium of cultural intolerance – indeed these are mostly inappropriate modern concepts. It is true that some cohesion was achieved through the extension of citizenship, but for the non-citizen masses of the early empire the differences in identities were real.

▶ Rebellions or revolutions?

During the long duration of the Roman empire, there were numerous major upheavals among its subject peoples. There were plenty of rebellions and several infamous military defeats, not least the annihilation of the three legions led by Varus in Germany in 9 CE. We will look at four of the most well-known upheavals in chronological order, one taking place in the late republic, the other three in the early empire. Significance lies not in the actual sequence of events in each case, but in the reasons for the outbreak of violence, the identity of the perpetrators and whether they were involved in a rebellion against temporary oppression or sought a total overthrow of the existing order.

Spartacus provides the first example. He was one of the leaders of a famous slave rebellion between 73 and 71 BCE in southern Italy, and his career has spawned its own heritage of sword-and-sandal movies, books, occasional artworks and computer games. Slaves often rebelled against oppressive masters, most often by absconding. During the final centuries BCE Italy was home to an enormous influx of captive slaves, taken during Rome's wars of expansion. Plutarch (of Chaeronea) provides a pen-portrait of Spartacus:

He was a Thracian from the nomadic tribes and not only had a great spirit and great physical strength, but was, much more than one would expect from his condition, most intelligent and cultured, being more like a Greek than a Thracian

(Plutarch, Life of Crassus, 8-11).

Note in passing that this is a standard authorial cliché: an explanation for the intelligence of any impressive 'barbarian' was always sought. Spartacus may have been trained as an auxiliary in the Roman army but he ended up as a slave-gladiator in the arena in Capua. His rebellion was momentarily popular (at its height the slave army numbered some tens of thousands) and successful (defeating Roman legions on several occasions). The slave army, however, suffered from an absence of clear strategic aims, and was ultimately routed in southern Italy. Roman reprisals were savage. Six thousand captives suffered roadside crucifixions, turning the Appian Way into an avenue of death between Capua and Rome. Two things are clear. First that Spartacus did not lead a revolution against slavery itself, and secondly the very public nature of Rome's revenge: the violent repression emphatically served to warn others not to follow Spartacus's example.

The next example concerns the rebellion of Boudica in southern Britain in 60–61 CE. After the Roman invasion of Britain in 43 CE, it is likely that the Iceni of East Anglia, ruled by Prasutagus and his wife Boudica, considered themselves allies of Rome and achieved, via treaty, the status of a friendly or client kingdom. The Iceni retained a notional independence, and many of their laws and customs, while enjoying protection from external attack. However the deaths of friendly rulers must always have been times of tension, since it was the practice of the emperor to sanction the new ruler. In this case it appears that Prasutagus, who died in 60 CE, was expected to nominate Emperor Nero as his sole heir; however,

▲ The statue of a defiant Boudica on the Embankment, Westminster Bridge, London.

he bequeathed half his estate to his family. Trouble was inevitable. The Roman forces committed many outrages, including the flogging of Boudica and the rape of her daughters. The Iceni mustered an army, attacking Roman towns such as Colchester, London and St Albans, as well as defeating detachments of the occupying forces. Ultimately Roman force of arms prevailed. Again retribution was immediate and arguably too repressive under the governor, Suetonius Paullinus: Iceni territories were taken under direct Roman rule, some of the population probably enslaved, and the lands possibly resettled by colonists. Nero eventually pursued a policy of appeasement and pacification, replacing Paullinus; peace was a requirement if tax revenues were to be maintained, and further conquests in Britain planned. Boudica eventually became a larger-than-life heroine, honoured with a statue on the Thames Embankment near London's Westminster Bridge in 1902.

The third rebellion, different again, is that of the Batavians, in present-day Netherlands, which took place in 69–70 CE. The Batavians were essentially a Roman construction, probably formed through a deliberate movement of a German people to the lower Rhine delta in the mid-first century BCE and their intermarriage there with the indigenous population. Known for their warlike characteristics, they were also skilled sailors, swimmers and horsemen. They had a special relationship with Rome, supplying units of auxiliary soldiers in return for exemptions from tax and tribute. The conscription of Batavian males, however, was onerous and estimates suggest that every Batavian household probably supplied at least one son to the Roman cause.

In the year 69 CE – the so-called year of the four emperors – the empire was convulsed by civil wars, with various legions supporting different candidates for the imperial throne; a period which ended with the triumph of Vespasian. The disorder and chaos provided the Batavians, under the leadership of Gaius Julius Civilis, a Batavian chief who had received citizenship – hence his Latin name – with the opportunity to rebel. The Batavians were assisted by other tribes and had some successes against Roman legions, but they failed to win over the majority of the peoples of Gaul. Once Vespasian had secured his ascendancy, the Romans regrouped, ultimately to defeat Civilis and the Batavians and impose humiliating terms, which included the destruction of their main stronghold and their forced resettlement to an indefensible location.

The reasons for the Batavian rebellion were probably multiple, but the miscalculated conscription of their youth undoubtedly was at the core of their unrest. In the words of Tacitus:

(*Tacitus*, Histories, 4.14).

Although Tacitus cannot have known what Civilis did say, the sentiments seem real enough. The Batavians came to feel that they had become slaves rather than allies.

The last example of rebellion is the great revolt of the Jewish people against Roman domination which began in 66 CE and ended in 73 CE. The initial spark for the rising in the Roman province of Judaea was apparently religious tension between Greeks and Jews in Caesarea, inflamed by the Greeks sacrificing birds in front of a synagogue in

66 CE. Protests against Roman taxation joined the list of grievances and random attacks on Roman citizens occurred in Jerusalem. The Romans retaliated by forcibly entering the Jewish temple claiming temple monies for the emperor. The Roman garrison was subsequently ousted and the rebellion quickly spread. The conflict went through many phases but ultimately was brought to an end in the siege of Jerusalem by the Romans under Titus in 70 CE. Most of the city was burnt, and the majority of its survivors sold into slavery. The famous Arch of Titus in Rome depicts Roman legionaries carrying the temple of Jerusalem's treasures, including the Menorah, during Titus's triumphal procession in Rome. The siege of the last Jewish stronghold, Masada – which the Romans surrounded with works of circumvallation – was finally successful in 73 CE. According to Josephus, when the Romans finally broke through the walls of this citadel in 73 CE, they discovered that 960 of the 967 defenders had committed suicide.

The reasons behind this sample of rebellions illustrate that the motives varied, although underlying them all was a phase of Roman oppression. They were not, however, revolutions in the Marxist sense of seeking a new order that would bring greater equality for the masses. They sought freedoms, but freedoms that were to be restored along lines that had existed in the past. A common result was the ferocity and public violence of the Roman reprisals: retributions intended not only to restore order in the present, but also to provide intimidating lessons for the future. All ancient states behaved in that way but Rome seems to have been especially ferocious.

▶ The city crowds

Roman 'civilization' was most pronounced in cities throughout the empire. The grid pattern of streets, the houses and public buildings, the civic amenities such as theatres and amphitheatres, and the religious monuments were meant to portray the ideal of cultured urban life. Yet the inhabitants of cities were largely drawn from the local population (non-citizens) and from slaves, with the occasional influx of discharged veterans, traders, new settlers and a few travellers. Clearly the peoples of the eastern half of the empire were much more used to city-life than those in Gaul, Spain or Britain. Linguistically the East was dominated by Greek, and the West by a sort of pidgin Latin, the *lingua franca* of the street. In reality the alleyways of each city must have echoed to a babble of different tongues and accents.

▲ The later Roman town walls of Chichester, southern Britain, complete with projecting bastions.

A fundamental characteristic of these city populations was that they did not constitute a collective blank canvas on which the colours of Rome could be painted and fixed. They possessed the customs and traditions of their homelands. In each city or town, therefore, there was an active mixing of inherited and adopted Roman lifestyles to forge new ways of doing things that were in part 'Roman' and in part indigenous, changing the cultures of both host and immigrant communities. This mixing of the old and the new produced novel identities, akin to the creolization that produced African-American cultures in the New World. These hybrid traits were also probably flexed to suit both occasion and gender. In public there may have been a greater emphasis on adopted Roman behaviours, in private on inherited behaviours. Women may have been more tied to local customs, men more receptive of Roman ones. Admittedly these are generalizations: there must have been plenty of exceptions.

Let us meet, all too briefly, some of these folk. Starting with the family: the Roman ideal for a reasonably financially comfortable family was the *domus*, which was a sort of extended household, containing husband (the *paterfamilias*), wife, children, slaves and possibly one or two freed individuals. Much Roman law concerned the transmission of property from one generation to the next. Significantly the wife was not considered part of the family. She could divorce her husband relatively easily, taking her belongings with her and having no claim on her husband's estate; nor he on hers. Slaves have already been mentioned, but their numbers were extraordinary.

In the first century CE they were likely to number about one fifth of the population. Slaves were either bought or were the offspring of slave parents. They could also be raised from the empire-wide practice of exposure of unwanted babies. There is evidence that in Egypt many foundlings were raised as slaves. Undoubtedly the lives of slaves varied in their degree of unpleasantness and degradation, but slaves were a 'given' of society. There is little evidence for any 'abolition of slavery' movement. Even the Christians accepted slavery:

> Slaves, obey in everything those who are your earthly masters, not with eye-service, as men-pleasers, but in singleness of heart, fearing the Lord

(St Paul, Colossians, 3:22-4:1).

Freed persons, ex-slaves of masters or mistresses, rewarded with liberty through the act of manumission, constituted another significant proportion of the population of any city. They often retained links with their former masters, and were given significant responsibilities, sometimes in trade and money-lending operations in which some of the elite disdained to become directly involved. Ex-slaves of the imperial family could rise to great heights in the empire's administration. The numbers of freed persons was certainly far less than the numbers of slaves, but large enough to draw some hostile comments from writers such as Juvenal. Successful freed persons in Rome who irked the metropolitan elite were assumed to hail from the eastern end of the Mediterranean. In the classic language of racial stereotypes they were accused of being effeminate and given to intrigue, and generally to be guilty of displacing virile and moral Romans. Fears of the effects of globalization, immigration and trans-nationalism thus have ancient pedigrees.

The most numerous category of people, both in cities and in the countryside, must have been the free and the poor: men, women and children living at subsistence level, whose lives were precarious and who were at risk from premature death, from natural catastrophe, plague, famine, illness and social disturbance, or from a change in other personal circumstances. Quantification is difficult but in an empire of some 60 million people they may have numbered 40 per cent of the population, perhaps some 25 million. The poor of the cities eked out a living in menial trades such as porters, messengers, day-labourers, cobblers, beggars and prostitutes. There was little Roman law directed at them, and many survived on their wits, scavenging and pilfering from the better off, and benefiting from the support of reciprocity amongst their kind. Nor did the poor necessarily strive to improve their future. For the great majority, like the slaves, the social conditions they lived in were accepted as their lot. Challenging and overcoming them, either collectively or individually, did not feature in their mental outlooks.

In some aspects there was some sort of equality; slaves, freed persons and the poor were not always distinguishable by dress or appearance. All of these people – let us take a guess at perhaps 40 million in total – were religious in the sense of believing in powers that ruled their lives. Depending on whether the individual was an urban or rural dweller drawn from an indigenous provincial population – as most of them were – or a resident of long-standing Roman towns such as Pompeii, they believed in the abilities of classical or native gods, or Eastern imported cults, to influence their lives. The Edict of Caracalla in 212 CE directed that all new citizens were expected to observe the festivals of Roman gods, but could also continue to follow their own particular deities if they wished. The common people relied on auguries, fortune-tellers or omens to predict their futures. Before the advent of an empire-wide Christianity in the fourth century CE, much worship was down to individual choice, eclectic and transactional: you made a vow in expectation of divine assistance. People's daily routines were laced with superstitious practices, with apotropaic rituals to ward off the all-seeing evil eye.

They were also equal in the potential respect and love they could both give and receive. The epitaphs on tombs are sometimes both surprising and poignant:

Celerinus, the master, set up this grave monument to the most unfortunate Valentina, his nursling and dearest delight, daughter of the slave Valentio, his steward, who lived but four years

(Corpus Inscriptionum Latinarum, 3.21 30).

▲ The extent of the Roman Empire around 200 CE.

And from a freedman butcher, Lucius, on the Viminal Hill in Rome, to his wife:

> *This woman, Aurelia Philematio, freedwoman of Lucius, who went before me in death, my one and only wife, chaste of body, faithfully loving a faithful husband, lived equal in devotion with no selfishness taking her from her duty*

(*Corpus Inscriptionum Latinarum*, 6.9499 = ILS 7472).

Whether people were freed, poor or slave there were bonds of affection and friendship that could lighten the constraints of enslavement or the rigours of subsistence livelihoods.

▶ Out in the sticks

The vast bulk of the empire's inhabitants lived in rural areas; perhaps as many as 50 million of the approximate 60 million total. These were very much the silent majority, perhaps with the exception of those who lived in classically influenced grand country houses we call villas. We know very little about them. Ancient authors only record them in passing, most often when there were political disturbances. Many of them must have continued their lives in ways that harked back to the period before Roman contact. Most derived their living from the land and their only real link to the great imperial administration was when the tax collector arrived to take tax in kind or in cash, or when called to register during a census. Some were free farmers, some were tied to the land by tenancies, others were possibly itinerant seasonal wage workers; some were slaves. In the first decades after the Roman annexation of southern Britain in 43 CE evidence from archaeology indicates that rural settlements continued much as before.

However, change did sometimes occur, perhaps made possible by the succession of generations, as new families of farmers emerged who had only known the world that these distant foreigners called Romans controlled. On the periphery of the provinces, such as the Rhine/Meuse delta, individual settlements consisted of clusters of traditional rectangular byre houses. These free families may have supplied auxiliary soldiers to the Roman army, and it was these on their return who introduced architectural elements such as roof tiles and stone cellars. These innovations stimulated hybrids that seem part classical, part indigenous.

Another example of this, higher up the social scale, is the appearance of double-courtyard villas in Gaul, Switzerland, Germany and Belgium. With one courtyard hosting elite dwellings and the other agricultural buildings archaeologists in the past frequently saw them as evidence for a pro-Roman local elite, drawing parallels with the type of villa described by Columella. However, recent research indicates that these type of villas are absent from other areas of the West, including Italy itself. Now they are seen as the successors of ditched enclosures with timber buildings that were developed by indigenous people. They do not thus represent a Roman imposition but rather a locally invented architectural form which selected and incorporated novel architectural ideas, especially regarding spatial layout. Such heterogeneous mixing of influences can also be found in temple and funerary architecture, and the naming of deities that combined local and classical names.

Instances of creolization can be detected elsewhere in the empire. In North Africa, a complex of elite tombs, dating from the late third and fourth centuries CE is concentrated around the rural village of Ghirza, some 250 km south-east of Tripoli. While well within the orbit of Roman administration the tombs display a mixture of Hellenistic, Punic and Roman traditions that suggest a creative acceptance of Roman overlordship. Some influences imported from Roman culture were delivered under very different circumstances. In the East, the Sassanians defeated a Roman army at Edessa in 260 CE, capturing the Emperor Valerian himself and 60,000 soldiers. These were put to work in the new city of Bishapur, east of the Persian Gulf, which was built on a square plan as befitted Roman practice, and not the more circular plan favoured by local architects. Many of these soldiers settled with local women, modifying both urban and rural lifestyles.

Countless societies developed, especially in rural areas, accepting what they wanted of classical culture, creating something new while retaining many of their local traditions. There must, however, have been many unrecorded instances of rebellion and resistance by local communities or individuals, villages or settlements: not against the might of Rome, or necessarily colonial domination, but more realistically against the pressure to increase agricultural yields, and to pay the higher taxes, that the imperial administrators demanded. There must also have been many small-scale acts of theft, or destruction of the landlord's goods, or feigned sickness or absence when workers should have been in the fields, or just instances of plain slander. These were everyday forms of peasant foot-dragging and resistance; they were the disguised weapons of the weak. As such, for the common people, they were much more successful than overt confrontations.

An empire of things

The Romans controlled an empire of people, but they also created an empire of 'things'. Indeed it is because of such 'things' that the Roman legacy is so obvious. By 'things' I mean all manner of material items, from the great buildings in cities throughout the empire, the rural villas and the new estates and patterns of fields associated with them, to the smaller objects of everyday life, such as coins, pottery and glass. There were special groups of things associated with different groups of people. The army had an extensive repertoire of fortified camps and structures of all different sizes and functions, and inventories of tools, weapons and armour. Merchants and traders could source supplies of different types of pottery and foodstuffs. The great and the good could erect statues in their honour, commission inscriptions to record their public-spirited benevolence, and erect tombs with eye-catching epitaphs to advertise their

▲ A hoard of 2,600 gold coins (aurei), concealed in a bronze vessel, and found in Trier in 1993. The earliest coins dated to 63 CE and the latest to 196 CE.

ival, even after death. And the borders of the empire ere permeable. The Romans imported exotica from as far away as southern India, and northern 'barbarians' bartered slaves for Roman goods.

So what is important about all this stuff, commonly called by academics 'material culture'? The sheer scale and variety, the different textures, shapes, colours and sizes from buildings to drinking cups marked a significant break from what was available before. Not everyone had access to them, but most people, sooner or later, encountered them. In the West particularly, where the range of material goods was more restricted before contact with Rome, local communities needed to work out their reactions to these novel things, and consciously or subconsciously decide whether to accept or reject some or all. Roman material culture was not neutral or inert. It carried with it ideas of how the civilized life of a Roman citizen might be lived. It could unwittingly proselytize, subvert traditional customs and convert people to a more 'Roman' way of life. If you were invited into a classically styled villa in Roman Britain, or walked along the main street of a city in Roman Africa, or enjoyed a meal in Roman Jerash, both your senses and thoughts were being moulded; you were being asked to consider the benefits that Rome could bring.

If this sounds a little too contrived there is some surviving written evidence that this particular power of Roman material culture was appreciated by classical writers, army leaders and traders, among others. We have already noted the celebrated description of Agricola's endeavours to entice Britons into the ways of town life and communal bathing, penned by the historian Tacitus. All those temples, togas, baths and banquets were knowingly introduced to the British elite to make them good Roman citizens. In an equally famous passage Diodorus Siculus remarked on the pre-conquest Gallic addiction for wine, which they drank un-mixed in a very un-Roman fashion. The traders played on this craving, receiving enormous rewards for the exchange of a single amphora of wine:

> *For in exchange for a jar of wine they receive a slave, getting a servant in return for a drink*
>
> *(Diodorus Siculus*, History, *V.26).*

Caesar seemed particularly sensitive to the power of the gift. Prior to his departure to Italy from Gaul he bestowed 'rich presents upon the principal citizens' (Caesar, *The Gallic Wars*, VIII, 49) in order to help maintain peace. Caesar had also noted that some 'barbarian' peoples recognized the potentially debilitating effect of Roman commodities. The Suebi allowed no wine or other luxuries to be imported, because 'they supposed that their spirit was likely to be enfeebled and their courage relaxed thereby' (Caesar, *The Gallic Wars*, IV, 2). These snippets of classical insight demonstrate that knowledge of the infiltrating powers of Roman 'things' was actively manipulated in parts of the empire.

The local communities that Rome sought to dominate (and then tax) were not necessarily willing recipients of imperial novelties and trinkets. Local chiefs and leaders, in the West, probably recognized the dangers of opening their doors to Roman material culture, while the kings of the much more ancient Middle East looked down with a certain amount of disdain on the things that the Romans brought with them. Local leaders reacted in different ways. Like the Suebi quoted above they could try to reject some or all Roman imports, or restrict them to a closed circle of the elite. Alternatively they could accept them, but in using them, give them a distinctly local twist. According to a rather cynical Athenaeus:

> *The Scythians and Thracians drink nothing but unmixed wine ... they pour it over their clothes and think that they practice a noble and happy custom*

(Athenaeus, Deipnosophists, 10.432).

For the southern Gauls too, wine was an alien form of alcoholic beverage that they quickly adapted to indigenous feasting practices.

There was a materiality about religion also: think of the temples, statues and myriad kinds of offerings. In religious observances a form of deity-twinning could be used to translate and perhaps entrap the gods of the conquering Romans. Throughout the Roman world classical gods were yoked to their local counterparts, a Sulis Minerva in Bath or a

Lenus Mars in Trier. Such strategies were open to ambiguous interpretations. They allowed indigenous priests to emphasize either local or imported beliefs, or a mixture of the two. In the north of Gaul some forms of Roman material culture seem to have been rejected. There some of the large amphorae – the pottery vessels that carried wine northwards from Italy and Spain – were deliberately broken in a way that suggests analogies with earlier sacrifices; the dismemberment of enemies which was carried out at indigenous sanctuaries. The red wine may have been spilt here to resemble blood.

Finally, the flows of material culture were not just one way. Certainly Roman goods flowed out from the great ports of the Mediterranean, but a lot of foreign goods found their way back to Italy. The enormous quantities of booty that were captured by Roman armies, especially during the expansionist wars of the late republic, have already been mentioned. In particular, some of the cities of classical Greece were ransacked for their artworks which were shipped back for the enjoyment of the Greek-speaking Roman elite. Emperor Hadrian's villa at Tivoli, in the hills east of Rome, was full of antiquities from Greece and Egypt. Exotic spices from the East, from places as far away as southern India, imported at great cost, could change elite diets in Rome. Goods were also imported from the West and the poet Catullus lamented the theft of his Spanish napkins, not because of their value, but because they reminded him of his friends who gave them to him.

Slaves, for the Romans, were 'things' too. Hundreds of thousands of foreign slaves were brought to Italy. Some reached influential positions. It would have been interesting to listen to the tales of the 'barbarian' north that the Germanic wet-nurse of the future Emperor Hadrian told him; perhaps she stimulated his lifelong interest in travel and different cultures. Some imports were distinctly healthy. Most Roman medical practice derived from the enslavement of Greek medical practitioners.

▶ Building future citizens

How did Roman buildings produce Roman citizens, or at least open people to Roman ideas? Let us start with a snapshot of two of its most well-known places, Rome and Pompeii. When in Rome, sooner or later, most visitors end up in the forum, or rather *fora*, and it often turns into a rather perplexing experience. This is because, rather than replace an old forum with a new one, Roman emperors sometimes added their specific forum alongside those of their predecessors. In a way this process mirrored the irregular phases of territorial acquisition that were accomplished by different Roman rulers, but it also emphasized the line of succession of various emperors, who claimed descent from favoured imperial predecessors. Ancient visitors to Rome, say in 120 CE, walking through the *fora*, with their proliferation of painted statues, triumphal arches and familiar inscriptions, must have felt they were taking a Roman history lesson. Who could not fail to be impressed by the structures and stories of successive emperors? And, to top it all, there was the nearby column of the recently deceased Emperor Trajan, recounting his crossing of the Danube and conquest of Dacia. If visitors did not immediately realize that they were at the epicentre of an ancient power with an unimaginable geographical reach, they certainly did by the end of their visit.

Travel down to Pompeii and at least the town is on a more easily understood scale. But wander around here and visitors can easily find themselves overwhelmed, not so much by the living as by the images of gods and goddesses. Pompeii was home to around 20,000 people but representations of divinities almost certainly outnumbered those of mortals. They came in all shapes, sizes and colours, from a painted, pin-up Venus – goddess of love, sex, fertility and victory – to miniature bronze figurines of the Lares; from deities of families' ancestors, to great marble heads of Jupiter, protector of the Roman people. These divine presences were meant to promote the welfare of the Roman state, the family, and personal wellbeing. Like other things material, religious influences could also flow two ways. The ivory figure of Lakshmi (Hindu goddess of wealth and prosperity), the miniature images of the dog-headed Egyptian god Anubis, and the worship at the temple of Isis attest to a pluralism of beliefs, some home grown, some imported. The presence of this divine Pompeian population shaped the lives of all the living.

But however much it might try, Rome could not impose a blueprint for urban buildings on all the communities that it incorporated within the empire. Certainly local elites were encouraged to adopt the forms of Roman buildings, and lay out their towns and cities, or adapt their existing ones, to conform to Roman ideals; but often they, and their building gangs, had their own ideas. We have already noted the courtyard villas of the West that, while superficially drawing inspiration from Roman examples, actually drew much of their organization from extant indigenous notions. This was a sort of architectural double bluff. Indigenous elites could both demonstrate to Roman overlords that they aspired to classical behaviours and claim to their subordinates that they held fast to tradition and custom. This architectural ambiguity may have allowed them room to adjust their posture as the occasion and times demanded. Multiple identities had their uses.

We can see these attitudes played out in the Roman cities of North Africa. Lepcis Magna, some way east of Tripoli in Libya, was an old Punic (Carthaginian) city that was brought within the ambit of the Roman control in the second century BCE when the province of Africa was created. Once part of the Roman world it appears that successive generations of Lepcis's elites vied with each other to fund and build some of the standard public buildings of the Roman cultural package. By the end of the first century CE a whole gamut of Roman-style buildings had been constructed, including an amphitheatre, theatre, basilica, market, nine temples, honorific arches, port buildings and a city wall. At first glance an observer would have thought that such a building programme represented a Roman takeover. But first appearances, then as now, can be deceptive.

In the case of Lepcis Magna it is noteworthy that despite the rash of Roman building, the old pre-Roman forum was paved after Roman control was imposed, and fully integrated into the city plan. In addition, well into the imperial era, the population still carried Punic names and Punic language was still being used in municipal inscriptions alongside Latin until the second century CE. It seems likely, therefore, that the elite of this city were content with some sort of dual identity, or a composite one in which local origins and Mediterranean-wide affiliations could sit happily side by side. Another interpretation could be that this phenomenon was a form of passive resistance to Roman authority, or that it flagged subtle differences between the private (Punic) persona and its public (Roman) counterpart. But even in public some Punic terms (such as *sufetes*) for elite office-holders were recorded into the second century CE.

In the ancient Middle East, where monument-embellished towns and cities had been established long before Roman domination, there are also indications that Roman encouragement to some urban landscapes resulted in only a veneer of classical construction. There are several distinct characteristics of these Eastern 'Roman' cities that demonstrate their indigenous architectural origins. Lengthy colonnaded and paved streets which featured in places such as Palmyra, Petra, Bostra, Gerasa, Philadelphia and Damascus have been interpreted in part as sacred, processional ways that were a characteristic feature of Eastern religious practice; it is easy to forget that Christianity began as an Eastern cult. Another point of discrimination between East and West concerns the predominance of *fora* in the latter, and colonnaded streets in the former. Some suggest that in these streets dwarfed by columns lies the origin of the bazaar street, at the core of many traditional Middle Eastern towns today.

The case studies purporting to demonstrate the overarching Eastern origins and styles of many towns and cities in the Middle East during the Roman period are numerous and complex. The underlying fulcrum of debate is rather more straightforward. Have generations of modern classical scholars, largely resident in the West, mostly keen to exalt the civilizing process of Roman imperialism, allowed themselves to be all too easily persuaded that the Eastern cities owe little to their indigenous origins, and most to their Greek or Roman contributions? The ambiguity of interpreting material culture means that the jury will be out for some time deliberating this proposition.

▶ It's the little things that matter most

The Romans created the conditions for one of the world's first consumer cultures. They were one of the first peoples to allow mass production in, for example, pottery, glass, bricks and tiles, bronzes, lamps, personal jewellery and foodstuffs. People before Roman contact desired things, naturally enough. But the sheer quantity, variety and geographical spread of artefacts made in the Roman empire dwarfed what had gone before. Why did these small things matter so much?

First, the power of small things was that they could penetrate the private, domestic space of the thousands of different communities, with their distinctive and un-Roman cultures, that lived within the boundaries of the empire. Visitors to a Roman city could gawp at the statues, scratch their heads deciphering an inscription or look in awe at the columned facade of a temple. But they could not take them home. Small things, however – the odd ring, drinking cup or pottery lamp – could be carried back to settlements and shown to neighbours. Secondly, these small things were an *agent provocateur* for Roman society. Once back in the rural settlement, that lamp or pottery dish provoked curiosity. How did they get that shiny finish on the dish, or that shape to the lamp, or that colour to both? What does that decoration mean? What do they eat off these dishes? How do they light the lamp, and with what? Where can we try this food, or get more oil for the lamp? It is easy to see how curiosity leads to a desire to acquire more, and how the repeated use of Roman objects in a 'barbarian' house led to a familiarity with at least a small segment of Roman lifestyles.

One thing follows another. In order to obtain more of these Roman novelties indigenous people needed to secure something to give in exchange. Sometimes this could be goods they produced at home – livestock, fleeces, grain; even human beings as potential slaves – but sooner or later they realized they needed coins, preferably Roman coins, to purchase the items. Once monetary transactions had been contemplated some of the traditional indigenous ways of acquiring objects, either through reciprocal gifting or bartering in kind, began to decline. The old ways were giving way to the new.

It is important to refrain from painting a picture of easily duped local communities, members of which were all too keen to get their hands on Roman bric-a-brac. Anthropological studies from around the world demonstrate that indigenous people, faced with pushy traders or shopkeepers from an oppressive colonial power, can be every bit as canny and choosy in their dealings as their colonial counterparts. Trickery, deception and subterfuge were not prerogatives reserved for Roman officials. We have noted already that some people may not have realized that these new trinkets were 'Roman' in the first place. Other native societies may have rejected them completely, or used them in a wholly un-Roman manner. Tacitus comments on the Germans:

> *One may see among them silver vases, given as gifts to their envoys and chieftains, but treated as of no more value than earthenware*
>
> (*Tacitus*, Germania, 5).

Alternatively, indigenous societies may have acquired Roman goods simply to exact vengeance, deliberately destroying them at the culmination of public rituals, discarding them in bogs or rivers, or burning them as offerings at shrines. The Romans or their agents – soldiers, merchants, landlords, tax-collectors, census-takers – were the subject of protest.

And what were these mass-produced Roman goods? Pottery was widely traded, especially fine wares such as *terra sigillata* ('Samian ware'), shiny red tableware produced in huge quantities at factory sites in Gaul and Germany. Pottery from Africa – known as African red slipware – was made in present-day Libya and Tunisia: again in shiny red fabrics and forms that included plates, dishes, bowls and flagons traded throughout the Mediterranean from the first to the seventh century CE. Foodstuffs were another significant item of

▲ A pair of samian bowls placed with an early Roman cremation burial in Chichester, southern Britain.

trade – olive oil, wine and a somewhat noxious fish-sauce called *garum* – these were exported and imported in vast quantities in large pottery vessels called amphorae. There is a huge dump of broken amphorae sherds at Monte Testaccio in the southern suburbs of Rome, near the Tiber, demonstrating the enormous quantities of oil (used for both cooking and light) imported for the city's inhabitants. The statistics for this ancient refuse heap are staggering: almost a kilometre in circumference, it is now 35 m in height and is estimated to contain sherds from some 53 million olive oil amphorae. Most of this trade was by sea and the ships needed cargoes of traded goods to take back on their return journeys. Egypt was a good port of call for importers to Italy since the Roman metropolitan masses needed vast amounts of grain for their daily bread. Even places as far afield as Britain could supply desirable goods in return. According to Strabo, writing early in the first century CE, Britain produced

> *grain, cattle, silver, gold and iron...*
> *hides, slaves and dogs*

(*Strabo*, The Geography, *IV, 5, 2*).

▶ 'It's the economy, stupid...'

This oft-repeated phrase was penned initially during Bill Clinton's successful run to the White House in 1992. It is relevant here if only to remind us that this is something the first emperor of Rome would never have said. The Romans of the early empire, including Augustus, did not have anything that resembled a comprehensive imperial economic policy, one that was supposed to improve general prosperity. However the Romans were mightily interested in the concept of taxation.

The most costly item of expenditure for the Roman coffers was the maintenance of the army, especially the paid army that emerged during the empire. Even back in the days of the republic, during the second Punic war, senators complained that the tribute of Sicily and Sardinia to Rome was being swallowed up by the cost of the armies there. When Rome interfered in Spain tribute was regularly sought from local communities to offset military expenditure. In Africa it was imposed immediately on the conquered in 146 BCE. Cicero called the tax:

A reward for victory and a penalty for having made war

(*Cicero*, Verres 2; 3.12).

An axiom of Rome's taxation system, during both republic and empire, was that the taxes recovered had to pay the costs of the standing army, as well as the additional costs of the imperial household, provincial governorships and public building programmes. In order to collect taxes the Romans used three principal methods. During the republic they auctioned off contracts to companies of tax collectors, thereby minimizing the risk of falling tax revenues. In the early empire, in provinces controlled by the emperor, they were collected by officials known as 'procurators'. In the later empire responsibility for collection lay with the local councils of provincial towns.

The kinds of taxes levied were many and varied. A tithe of 10 per cent was charged on land under seed, and on agricultural products such as wine, oil and fruits. There were taxes on property owned by Roman citizens. A second-century BCE decree from Cos indicates that little there escaped the taxation regime: firewood, prostitutes, four-footed animals, tunny fishing, incense selling and purple dyes were all liable. Poll taxes on adults were imposed. There were also numerous customs duties imposed on the transit of goods. These were charged at the frontiers of the empire or in particular provinces, at some bridges, city gates or major road intersections. The Romans were especially interested in gold, silver and copper bullion and significant provincial resources such as stone, iron or timber. Important revenues were raised from these sources either through tax or through direct management by Roman administrators. In the early empire people were encouraged to pay their taxes in Roman coinage or in kind. Tacitus records one instance of local revolt in Britain when the locals were forced to buy back grain, which they themselves had previously supplied, in order to pay taxes in kind:

For the provincials were made to wait outside locked granaries in order to go through the farce of 'buying' corn to deliver to the Governor – thus being

compelled to discharge their obligations
by money payments

(Tacitus, Agricola, *19).*

Where there were tax collectors there were tax dodgers. Tax evasion must have been widespread. In Roman Egypt a census was carried out every 14 years, and farmers quickly learned that if a field was fallow during the census year, then there was a chance it could be farmed and not taxed for the intervening 13 years.

By modern standards Roman taxation was low, and it has been argued that this encouraged general commerce and trading activity. However, the Roman authorities seem to have taken little direct interest in private enterprises, apart from taking their cut through taxing the movement of goods. In theory the Roman elite looked down their noses at anything to do with trade. In practice their involvement was disguised through the vicarious undertakings of loyal freedmen, who ran a primitive banking system and invested in profit-making schemes. The infamously satirised Trimalchio, a freed slave, bragged about his passion and success in business, and provides a distinctly pecuniary, perspective:

I built five ships, got a cargo of wine ... I
made a clear 10 million sesterces on one
voyage ... straightaway I built a house,
bought slaves and cattle ... I retired from

business and I began to lend money to
freedmen

(*Petronius*, Satyricon, 76).

In financial and material terms not all monies and goods connected with trade ended up in central Italy. There was a significant import of goods from the East, and particularly India in the first century CE, but an equally notable outflow of Roman hard currency to pay for it. According to Pliny:

It will not be amiss to set out the whole of the voyage from Egypt, now that reliable knowledge of it is for the first time accessible. It is an important subject, in view of the fact that in no year does India absorb less than fifty million sesterces of our Empire's wealth, sending back merchandise to be sold with us at a hundred times its prime cost

(*Pliny*, Natural History, 6.101).

These luxury items included a whole range of exotic goods: silk, pearls, precious woods and stones, ivory, textiles and spices such as cinnamon, pepper, cardamom, nard (an aromatic balsam) and cassia. Tigers and leopards may also have been imported, perhaps destined for the amphitheatres of Italy. Spices were the most pervasive import, enlivening many a meal for the Roman elite. Incense also played an important role in religious offerings and the cure of the sick.

The power of these commodities was seen by some in Italy as a corrupting one, leading conservative voices to complain how hard-earned wealth was being squandered on extravagances, encouraging sensuality and moral deprivation. The archaeological evidence for this commerce is relatively slight, although there are some finds of Roman coins and pottery in southern India. However, it would be a mistake to imagine Roman sailors and merchants stepping ashore on Indian soil. A few may have done, but most of the trade was effected by Indian and Red Sea middlemen, the goods being transferred from ship to ship. Nor must we imagine many fine diners in Rome discussing the geographical origins of some of the piquant flavours on their palates. For them knowledge of the whereabouts of the land of spices must have been hazy indeed. All that really mattered were the tastes, the novelty, and the ability to impress one's guests.

6

Decline and fall

Ever since Edward Gibbon penned those words in the late eighteenth century the 'decline and fall of the Roman empire' has been held up like a moralizing mirror, to challenge the worldly and the ambitious, to remind them of their fate. In Gibbon's view it was Christianity, and the barbarian incursions, that did for Rome. He thought that the Christian faith, attracting more and more adherents from the third century CE onwards, especially from the common people, undermined the previous beliefs in the Roman pantheon which upheld Roman authority and values. Christians thought more about the next world than the one they lived in, encouraging an excessive devotion to private salvation, rather than the public good, praising charitable donations rather than contributions to the public treasuries. According to Gibbon, the Roman empire also succumbed to barbarian invasions in large part due to the gradual loss of civic virtue among its citizens. They had outsourced their duties to defend their empire to barbarian mercenaries, who then became so numerous and essential that they were able to take over the empire. Romans, he believed, had become effeminate, unwilling to live a tougher, military lifestyle.

There is certainly much truth in Gibbon's identification of the Christian faith as a major factor in the disappearance of the Western Roman empire. But subsequent scholars have suggested other contributory causes. German scholarship has produced a list of over two hundred reasons why the Western empire disappeared. '*Christentum*' is certainly one of them, but also many others which are less convincing, such as '*Hyperthermia*' which leads to '*Impotenz*'. It is important to realize here that the decline of the Western empire was a long-drawn-out, uneven process, both chronologically and geographically. Indeed it is difficult to identify, even with hindsight, when things started to go wrong. The end of the Severan dynasty in 235 CE has more of a claim than most. And its end point? We will take the year of 476 CE, the date of the deposition of the last emperor resident in Italy, Romulus Augustulus 'the little Augustus'. It looks a highly significant act, but in reality the Western empire existed then in name only. Thus the decline took place over a period of nearly 250 years, ample time for myriad twists and turns of fortune along the way.

Two other points should be considered here. The first is that the multiple factors that combined to bring about Rome's fall acted in combination. We may not believe the above quoted example – that hyperthermia, brought about by too many visits to those overheated baths, led to impotence and thus to declining populations, fewer army recruits and tax-payers – but the idea that a concatenation of issues resulted in unintended consequences holds good. Second, it was the Western Roman empire that effectively disappeared in the late fifth century CE; its Eastern counterpart, centred on Constantinople, a city enlarged and inhabited by people who still called themselves Romans, would last far longer.

In what follows the detail is kept to a minimum, so we can concentrate more on the structural causes of the decline. Presenting the story chronologically is still probably the easiest way to appreciate how the nature of that decline, and associated factors, unfolded over the centuries. Salvian the Christian chronicler of Marseilles knew that the game was already up in the mid-fifth century:

▲ The extent of the Roman Empire, now confined to the east, in approximately 500 CE.

The Romans of old were most powerful; now we are without strength. They were feared; now it is we who are fearful. The barbarian peoples paid them tribute; now we are the tributaries of the barbarians. Our enemies make us pay for the very light of day, and our right to life has to be bought

(Salvian the Chronicler, The Governance of God, *Book VI, 18*).

The 'barbarians' will certainly feature, repeatedly, as one of the principal causes, but note in the above the shocking admission that where Rome had previously fought and conquered its enemies, now it paid them to leave Rome alone. Alternatively communities of 'barbarians' were settled within the empire's borders and their male offspring recruited to the Roman army, sometimes under their own commanders. The troubled and confused world of late antiquity was very different from the confident one of the first emperors.

▶ The third century crises

Let us begin at the top, with the emperors. The period from 235 to 284 CE was an age of violence that severely weakened imperial authority. Between 31 BCE and 235 CE there had only been 27 emperors, but in the next 50 years about 50 men received the title of emperor. Most were murdered by their soldiers or their generals. How could citizens of the empire have faith in government when one emperor was replaced by another with such frequency? The ambition of powerful men seeking to lead the empire resulted in frequent civil wars, which destroyed valuable manpower, swallowed up resources and brought great hardship for the local populations where the conflicts took place.

The northern frontiers of the empire were the most vulnerable; the Alamanni and the Goths began to make inroads. In the East the kingdom of Persia under the Sassanians emerged as a long-term threat to Roman interests. Foreign incursions could happen simultaneously, meaning that the emperor often had to move quickly from east to west or vice versa, necessitating long periods away from Rome. Unsurprisingly these empire-wide signs of disruption provoked secessionist movements. A Gallic empire was established by Postumus, governor of Lower Germany, in 260 CE, eventually incorporating Gaul, Spain and Britain. Concentrating on the defence of the Rhine, it survived for 15 years as a separate entity. Odaenathus of Palmyra, succeeded by his widow Zenobia, became virtual ruler of the East during the period from 260 to 272 CE. This followed the catastrophic defeat of Emperor Valerian by the Persians in 260 CE at Edessa (present-day Sanliurfa in south-eastern Turkey). Valerian was taken captive and never released, reputedly ending his days as a foot-stool which the Persian king used to mount his horse.

There were economic woes as well. In the republican period and the first two centuries of the imperial period revenue had been generated by taxes (kept reasonably low, around ten per cent), by booty, including slaves, from defeated enemies and by exploitation of natural resources. The mining of gold ore from which to make coinage was substantial. By the first century CE the gold fields of north-west Spain were contributing over six metric tonnes of gold annually, equivalent to about 85 million *sesterces* in value. However, for reasons that remain unclear, the scale of Roman mining declined markedly in Spain and other provinces after the second century CE. The gold mines of Dacia were relinquished when the Romans withdrew in the third century CE. In the later Roman period much more emphasis was placed on raising revenues by exacting higher levels of tax, by debasing the precious metal content of coinage, and by translating part of the cost of the armies into tax payments in kind. In the early first century CE the silver content of the denarius was 95 per cent; by 250 CE it had fallen to 40 per cent and by 270 CE stood at a paltry four per cent. The man whose image appeared on those coins – the emperor – must have been similarly debased.

Unsurprisingly, urbanism, the key foundation of classical 'civilization', began to suffer from the third century CE. It is difficult to summarize this phenomenon which varied in time and place. The towns of Britain, Germany and northern Gaul contracted first, while those in the Middle East survived much longer. In Gaul there seems to have been a concerted programme of urban retrenchment, related the barbarian threats, involving the construction of defensive walls enclosing much smaller areas, in the last three decades of the third century CE. Material for these walls was often secured not from quarrying but from the destruction and re-use of the town's monumental structures: so-called *spolia*. These reduced enceintes, or *castra*, offered secure bases for administration, grain stores and places of refuge. It is probable that the population of Rome also shrank dramatically.

For the third-century Roman citizen, then – and remember all of the empire's free inhabitants were now citizens – these were difficult times. The benefits of citizenship must have seemed more of a mixed blessing. Emperors followed one another in bewildering succession, civil wars were common, taxes were increasing, there was rampant inflation and an ever-present threat of 'barbarians'. Even town life did not provide the 'civilized' environment that it had once offered.

▶ The empire struggles back

A semblance of order needed to be re-established and it began in the 270s CE with the rule of Aurelian. An inscription in Rome records his victories over a series of 'barbarian' tribes to the north including the Iuthungi, the Goths, the Carpi and his capture of Zenobia in the East. A successor, Diocletian, acted on the widespread recognition that the empire could no longer be ruled by one person, and certainly not one person from Rome. The tetrarchy (from the Greek meaning 'rule of four people') became a successful experiment in power-sharing. By arrangements established in 293 CE, Diocletian was to rule the East, while his co-ruler Maximian was to look after the West. In addition two junior 'Caesars' were appointed, Galerius and Constantius, destined to succeed in the East and the West respectively.

The four rulers of the tetrarchy naturally enough needed four capitals, and it is notable that not one of the cities chosen was Rome itself. Nicomedia in Turkey became the Eastern base for Diocletian, while Sirmium, on the Danube near Belgrade, was home to Galerius. Mediolanum (modern Milan) was the capital of Maximian, and Trier that of Constantius. Trier in particular drew favourable comments in the late 380s:

...royal city of the Treveri, though full near the Rhine, reposes un-alarmed ... widely here walls stretch forward over a spreading hill; beside here the bounteous

Moselle glides past with peaceful stream,
carrying the far-brought merchandise
of all the races of the earth

(Ausonius, Ordo Urbium Nobilium).

The distribution of capitals was logical enough, designed to be nearer to the weakest frontiers, and the tetrarchs spent long periods leading armies in the field. It was not only enemies of Rome who felt the force of the tetrarchs. Spiritually the pagan gods of empire were revamped, and as a consequence, the followers of minority faiths such as Christianity suffered persecutions. Economic reforms also were undertaken including Diocletian's famous edict of 301 CE on maximum prices, designed to fix upper limits for commodities, services and wages, and attempts to stabilize the gold and silver content of the coinage. Rome was reserved for imperial rituals such as processions and triumphs, and for pleasurable pursuits – games and bathing – for which the gargantuan baths of Diocletian were constructed. The city had become a symbolic city of historical associations, religious observances and leisure.

The tetrarchy survived for some 20 years, when further civil wars eliminated most of the claimants to power, leaving Constantine in the West and Licinius in the East as co-rulers. Eventually Constantine fell out with Licinius, deposing him then having him arrested and hanged in 325 CE. With the demise of this first episode of power-sharing Constantine needed a symbol that would represent a new unity of West and East. The foundation of Constantinople (modern Istanbul) as a New Rome in 330 CE provided the answer.

Despite persecution of the Christians in the third century, when they were often used as scapegoats for military disasters and for a mid-century plague, Constantine abandoned intolerance in 312 CE and actively began supporting and promoting Christianity, not least through the construction of basilica-like churches in Rome. Debates still rage surrounding Constantine's motives. Was he a genuine convert? Was persecution too costly? Were Christians actually relatively popular? One thing Constantine discovered quickly was that the Christians were not united and he was soon heavily involved in trying to adjudicate between theological disputes and furiously schismatic Christian sects. Yet his patronage was pivotal and by the time of his death in 337 CE the position of the Church within the empire was unassailable.

If Constantine's vision was of a successful fusion between Christianity and imperial ideology he was to be disappointed. Paganism and Christianity still co-existed in the fourth century, although not always peacefully; witness the wanton destruction of pagan temples in the East:

These people attack temples with sticks and stones and bars of iron ... desolation follows, with the stripping of roofs, demolition of walls, the tearing down of statues and the overthrow of altars

(*Libanius of Antioch*, Speech *30.8*).

The senators of Rome were particularly tenacious supporters of the old gods. Christianity, on the other hand, was riven by heresy and schism, and simply did not provide any sense of cohesion across the empire. But although Christianity did not find slavery immoral, it did appeal to the common people, encouraging beliefs about charitable giving and sacrifice in this world and about salvation in the next. Whereas the pagan pantheon and the objectives of Roman imperialism had been largely in agreement in the early empire, the leading figures of the emerging Church sometimes seemed at odds with the wishes of the emperor.

Urbanism, the foundation on which Rome depended, was weakened still further by events of the fourth century CE. Euergetism, that phenomenon which encouraged the wealthy provincial elite to stand for local town councils and provide the wherewithal for the construction of the town's public buildings, gradually dissipated. The rich realised that the financial burdens of public office were becoming too great, so they spent more and more of their time and money on their rural retreats – the villas – especially in the West. The aggrandisement of the villa at Bignor in southern Britain is a good example of fourth-century investment by a super-rich landowner. The picture varies both regionally and locally, however. At the villa of Borg in Germany there is a decline in luxury in favour of economic activity in the fourth century, with small-scale industries taking place in some of the rooms. As a result the economic performance of cities and towns declined. If the elite spent money in towns at all it was on churches or private mansions. A good deal of provincial revenue was thus directed away from the public sphere and into its private or ecclesiastical counterpart. In the first two centuries of empire the propertied classes and Roman imperialism had worked together. Now, with the former disillusioned with the latter, they were diverging.

Despite the efforts of the empire, and its wars against the 'barbarians' beyond the Danube and the Rhine, and its campaigns to hold the Persians in check, the enemies of Rome were gradually becoming more formidable adversaries. Just as Rome, in the mid-republic, had learnt new military tactics and novel weapons from its foes, so the 'barbarians' now looked and learnt from what the Romans had to offer. The people now beyond Rome's borders had enjoyed generations of contact with the empire, either through trade, through military service as auxiliaries, or simply by co-residing in that fuzzy middle ground at the empire's limits. In essence there was little to choose between the fighting strengths and tactical expertise of armies on either side of the frontier. Roman military superiority was a thing of the past.

▶ Decline and destruction

If there is one date that signals an unstoppable acceleration of decline towards destruction of the Western Roman empire a good candidate would be 9 August 378 CE: the battle of Adrianople (near modern Edirne in European Turkey). Emperor Valens had fought a series of inconclusive wars against the

Goths. When the latter fled the warlike and nomadic Huns he allowed some of the Goths to settle in Roman territory south of the Danube as separate ethnic groups. Ammianus Marcellinus made it clear that the Huns were to blame:

The origin of all this destruction and of the various calamities are ... the Huns, who are ... quite abnormally savage ... with squat bodies, strong limbs and thick necks; they are so prodigiously ugly and bent that they resemble two-legged animals

(*Ammianus Marcellinus*, History of Rome from Constantine to Valens, *31.2.1-2*).

When the Goths rebelled Valens marched against them and suffered a serious defeat at Adrianople. The emperor died on the battlefield (his body was never recovered) and about two-thirds of his army (10,000 men) were slaughtered. The defeat was not an absolute catastrophe but it damaged Rome's military reputation, weakened her manpower, and most importantly it altered the balance between 'barbarian' and civilized, between Romans and Goths. The Goths and others knew, as they had done for some time, that Rome's borders were porous, that the empire could be challenged and defeated.

The 'barbarians' who increasingly swept through, and settled in, parts of the Western Roman empire in the first decades of the fifth century CE have not enjoyed a good historical press. All too often, and all too simplistically, the demise of the 'grandeur that was Rome' has been laid at their doors. *'What the Barbarians did for us'* makes a jokey strap line for a TV documentary on the Goths, Vandals and Alamanni, but the joke really forces us to consider whether our preconceived views are as balanced as we would like to think they are. One problem is that history tended to be written by the Romans who passed off hearsay and prejudice as a truth fit for a 'civilized' audience. A second problem lies in their names, their strangeness, their sinister overtones, and the fact that there were so many of them: Ostrogoths, Visigoths, Vandals, Greuthungi, Alamanni, Picts, Saxons, Franks, Gepids, Heruls and Alans, to name but a few. A glance at any historical atlas depicting the routes of these 'barbarian' migrations tells its own story. The Vandals crossed the middle Rhine in 406 CE passing through Gaul and Spain, eventually crossing to Africa in 429 CE and capturing Roman Carthage in 439 CE. The Visigoths, led by Alaric, moved through most countries bordering the north shores of the Mediterranean, even sacking Rome in 410 CE, ultimately settling in Italy and Spain.

These fifth-century 'barbarians', however, differed from some of their predecessors in one important respect: they did not want to destroy the empire. They wanted to co-operate with it; they wanted to become quasi-Romans too. Many of them adopted Latin, ruled with a continuance of Roman law, issued Roman coin types and maintained both urban living and the Christian Church.

The newcomers did not bring decay, but instead some stability to an already decaying order. For instance, the Ostrogoths at the end of the fifth century set up their capital at Ravenna, embellishing it with churches. Their king, Theodoric, was at the same time king of the Goths and unofficial successor of the last Western Roman emperor. Roman and Ostrogoth, differing in manners and language, lived side by side on the soil of Italy; each was ruled according to his own law, by the king who was, in his two separate characters, the common sovereign of both.

The Vandals, who also had managed to plunder Rome in 455 CE, established an African kingdom with its capital at Carthage. The ancient sources paint a picture of disruption and decline but more recent archaeological discoveries have challenged this assertion. In Carthage the street pattern remained the same and some public buildings and churches were renovated. Vandal currency was a creative adoption based on Roman models. New industrial centres also emerged within cities during this period. In particular the large amounts of African red slipware discovered across the Eastern Mediterranean dating from the Vandal period of North Africa strongly suggest that economic stability was maintained.

Given those lines of 'barbarian migrations' on the map it is hard to imagine anything like normal life still functioning, although it did, albeit in a faltering and worsening fashion. One area where the pinch was felt hardest was in taxation. It rose in the fifth century and records from Egypt show that a up to a quarter of the yield from agricultural land was now requisitioned. The tax requirements of empire were still enormous, with half the tax yield supporting the army, and another quarter paying for the *annona*, the corn and subsistence supply to Rome. In the West the gap between rich and poor increased: the rich could buy tax immunity corruptly but as ever the burden fell on the oppressed poor. Large numbers of slaves had been used to increase the agricultural outputs of landholdings in the late republic and early empire. Slavery of this sort had declined by the late empire, since the wars of conquest (resulting in slaves-as-prisoners) had vanished too, although slaves could still be produced by breeding.

If the poor were being pinched, the Western Roman empire as a political entity was taking one body blow after another. The sacking of Rome in 410 was a 9/11 event for the Western empire, sending shockwaves through the provinces. Britain's field army was recalled in 411, and peasant revolts continued for some 30 years in parts of central Gaul and Spain. In 416 one Senator emphasises the dangers of travelling between Rome and his battered estates in Gaul:

I will travel by water .... Tuscany and the Aurelian highway have already fallen to the Goths. It is best to trust the sea

*because the rivers are not bridged and
the land has become wild again*

(*Rutilius Namatianus*, De Reditu Suo, *1.3942*).

The Vandal take-over in Africa broke the link between Carthage and Rome, and specifically interrupted the major supply of grain and oil: the *annona*, taken as tax, that kept the citizens of Rome above the bread line. Quite simply, the Vandals wanted to control the agricultural produce for themselves. The population of Rome as a result went into steep decline after the mid-fifth century CE. From this period too taxation was probably insufficient to pay for imperial troops.

For the remaining decades of the fifth century Rome reeled as the breakdown of central government produced a growing separation of the regions of the Western empire. Where before there had been links, there were now ruptures. Archaeological evidence is clear too that the economic infrastructure and moneyed trading that had underpinned such an empire-wide proliferation of material culture – from architecturally outstanding public buildings to the pottery bowls, plates and glass goblets for fine dining – simply collapsed and the generations that succeeded adapted to timber buildings, barter and a greater use of wooden plates and leather flagons. The pace and characteristics of decline varied in the fifth century throughout the Western empire. It is thus difficult to put a finger on when the empire once ruled by Rome ceased, as such, to exist. Forced on this issue most scholars would plump for 4 September 476 CE when the last Western emperor, Romulus Augustulus, whose name echoed back to the founder of Rome and the founder of its empire, was deposed and replaced by a Germanic chieftain, predecessor of Theodoric, called Odoacer. The 'barbarians' were no longer at the gates of Rome; they were inside the city and it was their king who was on the throne.

▶ Historical epilogue

Those last few sentences could have been cinematic soundbites from the latest 'sword and sandal' product from Universal Studios. You can almost hear that thunderously portentous music ringing in your ears as you leave the cinema. But in reality it did not happen like that. By 476 CE most people who bothered knew that Rome's days as capital of the known world were long since gone. The great city survived but its governing pre-eminence disappeared with a whimper and a shrug of the shoulders. The last emperor of Rome was mockingly nick-named 'little Augustus'. He was a teenager, and had ruled for ten months. He was 'retired' to Campania where he must have been much happier.

In addition, despite the *longue durée* of the decline and fall it is important to remember that for ordinary people changes occurred slowly. An individual's appreciation of these events was one of slow transformation towards an unknown future, of a society and its communities gradually evolving. For sure times were getting tougher: rising taxes, increased demands for military service, fewer slaves, worsening communications, outbreaks of banditry, predatory military presences, inflation, higher costs of purchased goods, religious intolerances; these were the things that people worried about and which impacted their daily lives. There is ample documentary testimony of these fears:

It is a ruinous practice that the meadows of our provincials are being molested and harassed by the soldiers; encampments of troops must not unlawfully claim food or money from landholders

(*Codex Theodosianus, Laws of 364 and 415 CE*).

At the other end of the individual scale we can consider the position of the emperor himself. The empire had grown so extensive, its inhabitants so numerous and varied: how could one man possibly initiate and enforce empire-wide strategic policies, especially when communications were so slow and rudimentary? Surely the tetrarchy was an admission that the empire had just become too big for one man to govern? There is much to recommend this argument, and by and large it seems that the majority of emperors struggled with this challenge. There were exceptions, however; men whose vision, personality and commitment to Rome transcended the difficulties of geography and ethnic variability. The first emperor Augustus is a good example, and some of his successors – Hadrian, Marcus Aurelius and Constantine – stand comparison. Others have had their favourites.

Machiavelli in 1503 championed Nerva, Trajan, Hadrian, Antoninus Pius and Marcus Aurelius; Gibbon was also to select these five.

For many other emperors enforcing beneficial policies often proved problematic. Frustrated by provincial governors or town councillors who had their own views, or diverted by political intrigues in Rome or military campaigns abroad, or with messages simply ignored by rebellious generals in the field, what appeared as a good idea in the imperial palace on the Palatine often had unintended consequences. Standing back from the long trajectory of Roman conquests and imperialism – while never forgetting that it was an unjust and corrupt rule, frequently violently imposed on a scale not previously undertaken – Rome's troubles began when it stopped expanding territorially in the second century CE. Once the resources gained by conquest – the natural resources, the treasures, the influx of huge numbers of slaves – ceased, Rome had to manage what it held, within its limits. For a system of governance based fundamentally on an ideology of elite competition, often expressed in militaristic terms, this was problematic. The empire had stalled. The 'decline and fall' was the outcome of a progressive disentanglement, an unravelling, of people, things and ideologies over a period of three centuries. Separating out the individual threads has proven to be both a stimulating and inconclusive academic exercise. There is every chance it will continue to be so.

Romans living in the New Rome – Constantinople – prospered in the East long after 476 CE. Strategically located between Europe and Asia it became the capital of an Eastern Roman empire, becoming an extremely wealthy city. Constantinople too had its great emperors, including Justinian in the sixth century CE who attempted a reconquest of the lost Western half of the empire. The magnetism and resonance of Rome's achievements continued to influence many of Europe's leaders, and some thought to see themselves as the distant successors of the Western emperors. Charlemagne of the Franks expanded his empire from its base in north-west Europe to include parts of Italy and Spain. At Mass on Christmas Day in the year 800 CE, when Charlemagne knelt at the altar to pray, the Pope crowned him *Imperator Romanorum* (Emperor of the Romans) in Saint Peter's Basilica. The Holy Roman Empire of central Europe, founded in 962 and surviving until 1806, saw itself explicitly as the successor of the Western Roman empire. Its first ruler, Otto, was crowned Holy Roman Emperor.

While rulers in the West sought legitimacy and prestige through links with Rome, decisive ruptures were effected in the East through the Muslim conquests of the seventh and eighth centuries. The Middle East, North Africa and most of Spain were now ruled by caliphs who saw themselves as direct successors of the prophet Muhammad. Roman public buildings became quarries for the followers of Allah. Marble columns ripped from a Roman temple provided supports for the arches of the exquisite architecture of the mosque at Córdoba erected in its place. Islamic armies eventually overcame the rump that was left of the Eastern Roman empire. Constantinople fell in 1453, causing an exodus of Greek Byzantine scholars – poets, writers, musicians, astronomers, architects, artists, philosophers, scientists and theologians – to Rome and the West. Such an influx of learning provided a key stimulus to the development of Renaissance studies. But nobody during the Renaissance could have predicted, even with hindsight, one of its unintended and most trivial consequences: the proposed erection of a classically styled chicken coop in the Forest of Dean in the early twenty-first century CE.

10 Roman 'sword & sandals' films

The Eagle (2011) – in Roman Britain a young Roman soldier decides to honour his father by retrieving the legion's lost standards.

Gladiator (2000) – Russell Crowe, all mean and moody, seeks revenge on the emperor. Great music and opening battle scene!

Spartacus (1960) – Kirk Douglas as the slave leader – on the high ground literally and morally – leading a violent revolt against the decadent republic.

Ben-Hur (1959) – Charlton Heston as the Jewish prince, betrayed by his friend, and seeking revenge. Great chariot racing!

Caligula (1979) – Roman-themed soft-porn: all the decadence and depravity you could possibly desire.

Quo Vadis (1951) – a Roman general becomes infatuated with a female Christian hostage, leading him to question the rule of Emperor Nero.

Cleopatra (1963) – starred Elizabeth Taylor as Cleopatra and Richard Burton as Mark Anthony. Watch out for the asp!

The Sign of the Cross (1932) – Directed by Cecil B. De Mille, Nero fiddles as Rome burns then turns the heat up on the Christians.

Imperium – Augustus (2003) – Part history lesson, part soap opera: Livia (the wife of Augustus, played by Charlotte Rampling) schemes against her husband in favour of his stepson, Tiberius.

100 IDEAS

Julius Caesar (1970) – a film version of Shakespeare's play, re-telling events around the assassination of the Dictator.

10 Roman novels

The Wedding Shroud (Elisabeth Storrs, 2010) – about a Roman girl married to an Etruscan man in the events leading up to the war between Rome and Veii.

Scipio: A Novel (Ross Leckie, 1998) – second novel in a trilogy about the second Punic war.

The Shield of Rome (William Kelso, 2011) – set in 216 BCE in the aftermath of Rome's disastrous defeat at Cannae.

Spartacus (Howard Fast, 1951) – tells the story of the great slave revolt.

Young Caesar (Rex Warner, 1958) – recounts Caesar's early life up to the first consulate and the eve of his departure for Gaul.

The Tribune: A Novel of Ancient Rome (Patrick Larkin, 2003) – Lucius Aurelius Valens, a foot soldier in the Sixth Legion, witnesses a brutal act of carnage and soon becomes convinced that his superior officer is complicit.

I Am a Barbarian (Edgar Rice Burroughs, 1967) – the fictionalized memoirs of Caligula's slave, which, if the film is anything to go by, should be what is coyly referred to as 'racy'!

I, Claudius (Robert Graves, 1934) – a stuttering Claudius, who was a surprise choice for emperor, was immortalized by actor Derek Jacobi in the television adaptation.

Pompeii (Robert Harris, 2003) – a brilliant evocation of Roman Pompeii seen through the eyes of aqueduct engineer Marcus Attilius Primus.

Julian (Gore Vidal, 1964) – recounts the story of the emperor's life and his attempts to restore the old Roman pantheon, and crush Christianity.

10 divine deities

Jupiter – King of the gods. All the other gods were terrified of him and his weapon was the thunderbolt. Formed one of the Capitoline Triad, along with Juno and Minerva.

Mars – god of war and also an agricultural guardian. He was worshipped by the legions and the month of March was named after him.

Juno – protector of the state. She was a daughter of Saturn and also the wife of Jupiter and the mother of Mars and Vulcan. Juno also looked after the women of Rome.

Minerva – virgin goddess of poetry, medicine, wisdom, commerce, weaving, crafts, magic. She was often depicted with her sacred creature, an owl, a symbol of her wisdom.

Mercury – god who wore winged sandals and was the god of trade, merchants and travel.

Pluto – god of the dead. Allegedly Romans were afraid to say his name in case he noticed them and whisked them off to the underworld.

Vulcan – smith of the gods, who made Jupiter's thunderbolts. His smithy was in the fires of volcanic Etna on Sicily.

Cupid – god of love. His weapon was a bow and anyone hit by one of his arrows fell madly in love.

Apollo – god of the sun. Each day he drove his fiery chariot across the heavens to give light to the world.

Venus – goddess of love, fertility, sex, prosperity and victory. Born at sea, she was washed up on the shores of Cyprus in a scallop shell.

Nemesis – patron goddess of gladiators and hunters who fought wild beasts in the arena. She was seen as the goddess of revenge and avenger of crime.

10 top attractions in and around Rome

The Roman Forum – make sure you also visit the *fora* of Augustus, Nerva and Trajan, a little to the north of the main attraction.

The Palatine Hill – homes of the emperors, with the *Circus Maximus* to the south.

The Pantheon – words, pictures and even a virtual tour don't do it justice; you just have to go there!

The Ara Pacis – the Altar of Peace set up in honour of Augustus: this is the monument that symbolizes the transformation of the Roman republic into the Roman empire. Note the mausoleum of Augustus nearby.

Baths of Caracalla – the best surviving baths from the empire.

Hadrian's Mausoleum – better known as the Castel Sant'Angelo; turned by the Popes into fortress in the fourteenth century, and for operatic aficionados, the scene of Tosca's suicidal leap.

Colosseum – the archetypal monument that reflects some Roman values – for architecture, love of a spectacle and cruelty – and don't forget the nearby Arch of Constantine.

The Via Appia – walk along this Roman road south of Rome and be awestruck by the grandiose tombs which flank it, notably the imposing rotunda of Caecilia Metella wife of Crassus.

Ostia – a short train ride will take you to Ostia Antica, the port of Rome which flourished in the second century CE. Here you can appreciate a variety of urban buildings in what was a busy port, and a cosmopolitan home to a variety of immigrants from around the Mediterranean.

Hadrian's Villa at Tivoli – a bus ride from Rome and a must to visit. Hadrian created a spectacular series of architectural complexes, inspired by his travels abroad, especially to Greece and Egypt. The so-called maritime theatre, a residence within a residence surrounded by an oval moat, is the ultimate imperial retreat.

10 top attractions outside Rome

Pompeii – the best preserved and most extensive Roman town, thanks to the eruption of Vesuvius.

Herculaneum – close to Pompeii but exceptionally good in providing an idea of the upper storeys of Roman town houses.

Lepcis Magna, Libya – the home town of Rome's first African emperor, Septimius Severus.

Pula, Croatia – famed for its magnificent amphitheatre, built at the time of Augustus. The corridors beneath the arena which were once paced by gladiators now house grape and olive presses and amphorae.

Jerash, Jordan – the so-called Pompeii of the East, the paved and colonnaded streets provide a memorable experience of an Eastern Roman city.

Conimbriga, Portugal – the best-preserved Roman town in Portugal. Excellent for its mosaics.

Housesteads Fort, England – a great place to see the layout of a complete Roman fort and to walk along an adjoining section of Hadrian's Wall.

Xanten, Germany – one of the largest archaeological parks in the world based on the various Roman settlements at the site. The practice of reconstructing some of the ancient buildings and fortifications aids understanding.

Trier, Germany – situated on the banks of the delightful Moselle; various Roman sites in the town, including Baths and the Basilica, and the famous Porta Nigra, as well as an excellent museum, make this town a must.

Ephesus, Turkey – a magnificent urban site that tells the complete story of Rome in the East. A Greek, Hellenistic, Roman and Byzantine town.

10 poisonous pen-portraits of emperors

Caligula (37–41) – He was very tall and extremely pale, with an un-shapely body, but very thick neck and legs ... his hair was thin and entirely gone on the top of his head, though his body was hairy (*Suetonius*).

Nero (54–68) – After Claudius's death he vented on him every kind of insult, in act and word, charging him now with folly and now with cruelty; for it was a favourite joke of his to say that Claudius had ceased to play the fool among mortals... and he disregarded many of his decrees and acts as the work of a madman (*Suetonius*).

Domitian (81–96) – He was so sensitive about his baldness that he regarded it as a personal insult if anyone else was suggested as bald, even in jest or earnest (*Suetonius*).

Commodus (180–92) – Our history now descends from a kingdom of gold to one of iron and rust, as affairs did for the Romans of that day (*Cassius Dio*).

Caracalla (211–17) – He was gluttonous in his use of food and addicted to wine, hated by his household and detested in every camp save that of praetorian guard; and between him and his brother there was no resemblance whatever (*Historia Augusta*).

Macrinus (271–81) – He was a Moor by birth from Caesarea ... so that he was very appropriately likened to an ass; in particular, one of his ears had been pierced in accordance with the custom followed by most of the Moors (*Cassius Dio*).

Elagabalus (281–22) – He had planned to cut off his genitals altogether ... the circumcision he actually carried out was part of the priestly requirements of Elagabalus, and he accordingly mutilated many of his companions in like manner (*Cassius Dio*).

Maximinus Thrax (235–38) – For Gaius Iulius Maximinus, commander of Trebellica, was the first of the ordinary soldiers who, though almost illiterate, seized power with the votes of the legions (*Aurelius Victor*).

Amelius Aemilianus (253) – Aemilianus came from an extremely insignificant family, his reign was even more insignificant, and he was slain by his own soldiers in the third month (*Eutropius*).

Diocletian (284–305) – Diocletian was an author of crimes and a deviser of evil; he ruined everything and could not keep his hands from God. He appointed three men to share his rule...multiplying the armies ... since each strove to have a far larger number of troops (*Lactantius*).

10 digital resources – for learning and fun!

Britannica Kids: Ancient Rome – perfect app for exploring the rich history of Ancient Rome. Learn all about the fascinating rise of the Roman empire, the Caesars, the gladiators and the Roman republic in fun, engaging and interactive ways.

Populus Romanus – an app featuring a turn-based strategy war game where you lead Roman legions against different tribes in their conquest of the Italian peninsula in 396 BCE. Play various scenarios of the conflicts fought by the Roman republic.

Populus Romanus 2: Britannia – your chance to tackle Boudica: an app featuring a turn-based strategy war game where you return to ancient Rome, this time leading Roman legions against British tribes in their conquest of the island of Britannia.

www.roman-emperors.org/ – an online encyclopaedia of Roman rulers and their families.

www.mrdowling.com/702rome.html/ – Mr Dowling's Electronic Passport to The Romans – helps kids browse the Roman world in a virtual classroom.

www.museumoflondon.org.uk/learning/features_facts/ digging/index.html – This Museum of London site for students explores Roman London and Britain through archaeological remains. It is organized around six major themes: People, Town Life, Invasion and Settlement, Army, Beliefs and Crafts, Roads and Trade.

www.perseus.tufts.edu/hopper/ – Perseus Project is an impressive digital library for Greek and Classical resources from the Classics Department at Tufts University for primary and secondary source scholarly works that cover the history, literature and culture of the Greco-Roman world.

www.roman-empire.net/ – This website offers a comprehensive history of the Roman Empire through essays, chronologies, photo galleries, maps, lists, timelines, and more. Major categories include The Founding, The Kings, The Republic, Early Emperors, The Decline, The Collapse, Constantinople, Religion, Society, and The Army.

www.britishmuseum.org/explore/cultures/europe/ancient_rome.aspx – From the British Museum this is an introduction to ancient Rome. You are invited to explore the world of the Romans through various Roman objects.

http://byzantium.seashell.net.nz/ – The Byzantine Empire bridged the gap between the Romans and early modern Europe. From its inception as the eastern half of the partitioned Roman Empire in the fourth century CE through to its final disappearance in the fifteenth century, Byzantium played the role of an economic, political, and cultural superpower.

10 great classical writers and examples of their works

Julius Caesar (100–44 BCE) – wrote Commentarii de Bello Gallico, usually known in English as The Gallic Wars, seven books each covering a year of his campaigns in Gaul and southern Britain in the 50s BC.

Cicero (106–43 BCE) – wrote on society, government and philosophy; major works include De Re Publica (On The Republic) and De Legibus (On The Laws).

Livy (59 BCE–17 CE) – a Roman historian who wrote a monumental history of Rome and the Roman people.

Virgil (70–19 BCE) – a poet of the Augustan period. He is known for three major works of Latin literature, the Eclogues (or Bucolics), the Georgics, and the epic Aeneid.

Juvenal (late first/early second century CE) – Roman poet and author of the Satires, a helpful source for studying the culture of early imperial Rome.

Tacitus (56–117 CE) – senator and historian of the Roman empire. The surviving portions of his two major works – the Annals and the Histories – examine the reigns of the Roman emperors Tiberius, Claudius, Nero, and those who reigned in the year of the four emperors (69 CE).

Suetonius (c. 69–c. 122 CE) – a Roman historian belonging to the equestrian order who wrote during the early imperial era of the Roman empire. His most important surviving work is a set of biographies of twelve successive Roman rulers, from Julius Caesar to Domitian, entitled De Vita Caesarum.

Cassius Dio (c.150–235 CE) – Roman consul and noted historian who wrote in Greek. Dio published a history of Rome in 80 volumes, beginning with the legendary arrival of Aeneas in Italy.

Pliny the Younger (61–112 CE) – lawyer, author, and magistrate of Rome. He witnessed and described the eruption of Vesuvius in 79 CE. Pliny wrote hundreds of letters, many of which still survive. They are regarded as a valuable historical source for the time period.

Ammianus Marcellinus (fourth century CE) – his work chronicled in Latin the history of Rome from 96 to 378, although only the sections covering the period 353–378 are extant.

10 great battles

The Battle of Lake Regillus (498 BCE) – a quasi-legendary early Roman victory, won over the Latin League led by the expelled Etruscan former king of Rome.

The Siege of Veii (396 BCE) – the Romans finally sacked the Etruscan town, reputedly digging a tunnel under the city's walls and emerging inside it via the temple of Juno.

The Battle of Zama (202 BCE) – marked the final and decisive end of the second Punic war. A Roman army led by Publius Cornelius Scipio Africanus defeated a Carthaginian force led by the celebrated commander Hannibal.

The Battle of Corinth (146 BCE) – resulted in the complete and total destruction of the state of Corinth which was previously famous for its fabulous wealth. This battle marked the beginning of a new age in Greek history known as Roman Greece.

The Battle of Carrhae (53 BCE) – a crushing defeat at the hands of the Persians. Led to the death of the Roman commander Crassus, and the collapse of the first triumvirate.

The Battle of Actium (31 BCE) – a decisive naval engagement off Greece that gave Octavian victory over Anthony and Cleopatra, paving the way for the establishment of the imperial period of Rome's history.

The 'Battle of Watling Street' (61 CE) – the rebel forces of Boudica are finally defeated in central Britain by Roman legions under the control of Suetonius Paulinus. The actual location of the battle site is not known.

The Siege of Sarmizegetusa (106 CE) – between the army of the Roman Emperor Trajan, and the Dacians led by King Decebalus. A record of the victory and the destruction of the Dacian capital was depicted on Trajan's Column in Rome.

The Battle of Edessa (260 CE) – between the armies of the Roman empire under the command of Emperor Valerian and Sassanian forces under Shahanshah (King of the Kings) Shapur I. The Roman army was defeated and captured in its entirety by the Persian forces, including Valerian himself.

The Battle of Adrianople (378 CE) – was fought between the Roman Emperor Valens and Gothic rebels led by Fritigern. It ended in an overwhelming victory for the Goths.

10 memorable Roman quotations or phrases.

Audentis fortuna iuvat (Virgil) – Fortune favours the brave.

Amor vincit omnia (Virgil) – Love conquers all things.

Carpe diem (Horace) – Seize the day.

Errare humanum est (Seneca the Younger) – To err is human.

Cave Canem (Mosaic from Pompeii) – Beware of the dog.

Ut sementem feceris, ita metes (Cicero) – As you sow, so you shall reap.

Festina lente (Augustus) – Make haste slowly.

Veni, vidi, vici! (Julius Caesar) – I came, I saw, I conquered.

Cum grano salis (Pliny the Elder) – With a grain of salt.

Alea iacta est (Caesar) – The die has been cast.

Author biography

John Manley is an archaeologist who has excavated widely around the world, including sites in Italy, the Caribbean, Ethiopia, South Africa, Iran and Afghanistan, as well as in Western Europe and the UK. His most notable excavations on Roman sites have been at Fishbourne Roman Palace (Chichester, UK) the probable residence of a client or friendly king during the Roman annexation of southern Britain, and at Jerash (ancient Gerasa) in Jordan. He was CEO of the Sussex Archaeological Society, the largest county archaeological society in the UK, for 16 years. As well as holding a research degree in archaeology, he also has a strong interest in social anthropology, and holds a PhD in that field, applying the insights of anthropology to Roman archaeology. He is the author of numerous articles and several books, including *The Atlas of Past Worlds* (Cassell, 1993),*The Roman Invasion of Britain* (Tempus, 2001), *The Archaeology of Fishbourne and Chichester* (Lewes, 2008) and most recently *An Introduction to the Archaeology of the South Downs National Park* (Lewes, 2012). He is currently the Honorary Research Fellow of the Sussex Archaeological Society.

Select bibliography

There is a vast literature on the Romans, and the small selection below provides a sample of some of the most recent publications (Gibbon excluded). Each of these books contains an extensive bibliography which can be used to source further information and references. The book by Mellor (2012) provides an excellent introduction to the principal classical authors who recorded the history of Rome. More comprehensive coverage is provided by the authoritative volumes of the *Cambridge Ancient History*: see especially volumes 7 to 14. Key journals are the *Journal of Roman Studies* and the *Journal of Roman Archaeology*.

Texts for most of the ancient sources cited can be found in such collections as the Loeb Classical Library of Harvard University, or online sources such as the Perseus Digital Library at Tufts University (http://www.perseus.tufts.edu/hopper/).

Ball, W., *Rome in the East* (London: Routledge, 2000)

Beard, M., *Pompeii* (London: Profile Books, 2008)

Bringmann, K., *A History of the Roman Republic* (Cambridge: Polity Press, 2007)

Campbell, B., *The Romans and their World* (London: Yale University Press, 2011)

Christie, N., *The Fall of the Western Roman Empire* (London: Bloomsbury, 2011)

Flower, H. I. (ed.), *The Cambridge Companion to the Roman Republic* (Cambridge: Cambridge University Press, 2004)

Gibbon, E., *The Decline and Fall of the Roman Empire* (Hertfordshire: Wordsworth Editions, 1998 [1776-1788] (abridged))

Goldsworthy, A., *The Complete Roman Army* (London: Thames & Hudson, 2003)

Gwynn, D. M., *The Roman Republic: A Very Short Introduction* (Oxford: Oxford University Press, 2012)

Kelly, C., *The Roman Empire: A Very Short Introduction* (Oxford: Oxford University Press, 2006)

Kennedy, D., *Gerasa and the Decapolis* (London: Duckworth, 2007)

Knapp, R., *Invisible Romans* (London: Profile Books, 2011)

Mattingly, D. J., *Imperialism, Power and Identity – Experiencing the Roman Empire* (New Jersey: Princeton University Press, 2011)

Mellor, R., *The Historians of Ancient Rome* (London: Routledge, 2012 (2nd edition))

Morley, N., *The Roman Empire* (London: Pluto Press, 2010)

Rogers, G. M., Millar, F. and Cotton, H. (eds), *Fergus Millar's Rome, the Greek World, and the East: The Landmark 3-Volume Set That Transformed The Study Of The Roman Empire.* (Chapel Hill: University of North Carolina, 2011 (Kindle Edition))

Sears, G., *The Cities of Roman Africa* (Stroud: The History Press, 2011)

Ward-Perkins, B., *The Fall of Rome* (Oxford: Oxford University Press, 2005)

Warrior, V. M., *Roman Religion* (Cambridge: Cambridge University Press, 2006)

Wickham, C., *The Inheritance of Rome* (London: Penguin Books, 2010)

Woolf, G. (ed.), *The Cambridge Illustrated History of the Roman World* (Cambridge: Cambridge University Press, 2003)

Woolf, G., *Rome – an Empire's Story* (Oxford: Oxford University Press, 2012)

Index

153

ALL THAT MATTERS: THE ROMANS

Acknowledgements

The author would like to thank the following colleagues who interrupted their Christmas 2012 festivities to read and comment on an earlier typescript: David Kennedy, Warwick Ball, David Thompson, Ernest Black, David Bird and Mark Hassall. Their comments were invaluable and the text immeasurably improved as a result. He also acknowledges his immense debt to innumerable scholars, past and present, of the Roman period, a few of whose works appear in the bibliography. Not forgetting his agent, Frances Kelly, whose talent for putting publisher and author together has always been astute.

Timeline

BCE	The Roman republic
753–510	The regal period of Roman history.
509	Rome's first treaty with Carthage and the foundation of the republic.
396	Traditional date for the destruction of Veii by Rome.
390	Traditional date for the Gallic sack of Rome.
343–290	Rome frequently at war with the Samnites of central Italy.
336–323	Reign of Alexander the Great of Macedon, conqueror of Greece and the Persian empire.
264–241	The first Punic war, resulting in the defeat of Carthage and the annexation of Rome's first overseas province, Sicily.
218–201	The second Punic war, during which Hannibal inflicts Rome's most serious defeat at Cannae.
197 onwards	Rome has increasing involvement in Greece and the Middle East.
149–146	Third Punic war ends in destruction of Carthage; destruction of Corinth.
133	Rome captures Numantia in Spain; Attalus III of Pergamum (present-day western Turkey) dies, leaving his kingdom to Rome.
125–122	Roman armies in southern Gaul.
89	Mithridates of Pontus (northern Turkey) invades Asia, ultimately crossing to Greece; Rome loses control over all territory east of the Adriatic.
59–53	Caesar proclaimed consul and conquers Gaul, with raids into southern Britain and Germany.
44	Caesar assassinated on the Ides (15th) of March by a conspiracy of senators.
31	Octavian defeats Antony and Cleopatra, ending the civil wars.
27	Octavian is honoured with the title Augustus by the Senate.

CE	The Roman empire
14	Death of Augustus, the first emperor.
69	Year of the four emperors ends with Vespasian victorious and the establishment of the Flavian dynasty.
117–138	Reign of Hadrian; building of Hadrian's Wall and organized Roman withdraw from Mesopotamia (present-day Iraq).

165–180	Plague sweeps westwards across the empire.
212	Emperor Caracalla grants Roman citizenship to all free males; all free women in the empire are given the same rights as Roman women.
235	Death of Alexander Severus marks the end of the Severan dynasty.
250s	Increasing raids across the Rhine by the Alamanni and other groups.
260	Capture and execution of Emperor Valerian by the Persians.
284	Accession of Emperor Diocletian.
313	Emperor Constantine's *Edict of Toleration* legalizes Christianity across the empire.
376	Emperor Valens allows groups of Goths to cross the Danube, initiating a chain of events that leads to the defeat of a Roman army at Adrianople.
409–475	Gradual conquest of Iberian peninsula by Visigoths
410	Sack of Rome by the Goths. Emperor Honorius withdraws field army from Britain.
439	Capture of Carthage by the Vandals.
455	Rome sacked by the Vandals.
476	Last Western emperor, Romulus Augustulus, deposed by Odoacer the Ostrogoth.